The Flying Grocer

To Elva

To Peter
love Ray
& Christine

The Flying Grocer

RUPERT GUINNESS

RANDOM HOUSE AUSTRALIA

Random House Australia Pty Ltd
Level 3, 100 Pacific Highway, North Sydney, NSW 2060
www.randomhouse.com.au

Sydney New York Toronto
London Auckland Johannesburg

First published by Random House Australia 2007

National Library of Australia
Cataloguing-in-Publication Entry

Guinness, Rupert.
The flying grocer.

ISBN 978 1 74166 531 4.

1. Bennett, Keith. 2. Australia. Royal Australian Air
Force. Squadron, 460 – History. 3. Australia. Royal
Australian Air Force. Squadron, 460 – Biography. 4. Bomber
pilots – Australia – Biography. 5. World War, 1939–1945 –
Netherlands – Aerial operations, Australian. I. Title.

940.5449492

Cover design by Darian Causby/Highway 51 Design Works
Internal design by Midland Typesetters
Typeset in Palatino by Midland Typesetters, Australia
Printed and bound by Griffin Press, South Australia

10 9 8 7 6 5 4 3 2 1

Contents

Preface

ALTHOUGH THE STORY OF THE 'Flying Grocer' is a story from war, it is not a war story. Instead, it is a human story that aims to highlight the good in people rather than the bad – albeit in horrific circumstances.

This story is based on several people's experiences of one of the greatest humanitarian missions ever carried out in a time of war – Operation Manna, the food-drop over western Holland in April–May 1945 that saved millions of Dutch lives. Manna is the Biblical moniker referring to the food God 'gave' to the Israelites during their journey through the desert.

This particular tale no doubt mirrors the experiences of hundreds of thousands of others who were involved in the operation at the time. Nevertheless, it is a story worth telling if this humanitarian operation is to receive the recognition it deserves.

The Flying Grocer recounts many of the battle experiences of Flying Officer Keith Bennett DFC, his six crew and others of the Royal Australian Air Force's fabled Australian 460 Squadron in World War II, but by no means do I intend to glorify the death and devastation of the war – and in this case, the carnage and destruction wrought by the Bomber Command to which 460 Squadron had been attached to serve with distinction.

The recollections in these pages of the battles and hardships endured – together with the suffering of the Dutch while under German occupation – aim to provide a clearer understanding of why those like Bennett valued the chance to end the war by participating in Operation Manna; and similarly, why so many of the Dutch, like Jannie Verstigen (née Van Splunder), were so grateful and indebted for the rest of their lives.

It is a miracle of sorts that the two principal subjects – Bennett and Verstigen – ever came in contact with each other, let alone met and eventually became life-long friends. Bennett, like many war veterans, hated the war and would never speak of it. And while he sadly passed away on 25 February 2004 with his inner thoughts eternally under lock and key, I hope that his diaries and RAAF logbook, Verstigen's first-hand recollections, their correspondence, the thoughts of Bennett's surviving crew and friends, and the families of all parties, combine to paint a vivid picture of these extraordinary events.

However, any account of this story would be incomplete without a reminder of the heavy price and sacrifice it wrested during World War II. And not only by the hundreds of thousands of Dutch people who starved and died under the Nazi occupation, but by 460 Squadron that played such an integral role in Bomber Command. As Air Chief Marshal Angus Houston AO, AFC, Chief of the Defence Force (Australia) wrote in a letter to Flying Officer Bennett's wife Elva after he passed away: 'Your husband represents to me the great generation of the Royal Australian Air Force who laid the foundations for the organisation we are today. As a member of 460 Squadron, no group of Australians did more to win the air war in Europe – they flew the most sorties, dropped the most bombs, were awarded the most decorations, and sadly, lost the most lives of all Bomber Command units.'

It is fitting that a squadron held in such esteem was so integral to the success of Operation Manna. When history refers to 460 Squadron, it so often describes its major role in the massive bombing raids over Germany. Less known is their indelible mark on what was one of the greatest humanitarian missions ever conducted in modern war. I hope that *The Flying Grocer* makes this contribution somewhat clearer.

Rupert Guinness

460 Squadron

Bombing missions: 12 March 1942–25 April 1945
Formed: 1 November 1941 at Molesworth
Disbanded: 2 October 1945 at East Kirkby
Total number of sorties: 6264
Tonnage of bombs dropped: 24,846
Operational hours flown: 30,526
Enemy aircraft destroyed: 7
Enemy aircraft damaged: 34
Enemy aircraft probably destroyed: 6
Squadron aircraft lost on Ops: 181
Squadron aircraft lost in training: 7
Aircrew killed or died of wounds: 978

Decorations
Distinguished Service Order (DSO): 9
Distinguished Flying Cross (DFC): 228
Bar to DFC: 14
Conspicuous Gallantry Medal (CGM): 1
Distinguished Flying Medal (DFM): 101
Member of the Order of the British Empire (MBE): 1
Distinguished Conduct Medal (DCM): 1
Mentioned-in-Dispatches: 8

Above statistics from Strike and Return *by Peter Firkins*

Foreword

I was deeply saddened when I learned in March 2004 that Keith Bennett had passed away. The Royal Australian Air Force (RAAF) had lost yet another of its great Second World War generation, and I felt compelled to express my sympathy to Keith's widow, Elva. Though I never had the pleasure of meeting Keith myself, I – along with nearly every past and current serving member of the RAAF – certainly knew a great deal about his wartime achievements as one of the staunchly courageous men of 460 Squadron.

The feats of 460 Squadron during the Second World War and the valour of her crews remain an inspiration for those of us serving today. The squadron formed part of Bomber Command – the Allies' most effective means of striking directly at Germany. Within Bomber Command, 460 Squadron played a crucial role in destroying German targets and supporting the advancing Allied armies. 460 Squadron flew more sorties than any other Australian bomber squadron and they dropped more bomb tonnage than any squadron in the whole of Bomber Command.

However, as is most often the case in wartime, their great achievement came with great sacrifice. Casualties in Bomber Command were so high that a crew had only a 50 per cent chance of surviving one tour. 460 Squadron alone lost 1018 men – effectively wiping out the squadron five times over.

Flying Officer Keith Bennett was a pilot with 460 Squadron. The story contained in the pages of this book is his story, told with remarkable insight by his son-in-law Rupert Guinness. *The Flying Grocer* tells us of Keith's great courage, stamina, dedication and skill during his time flying Lancasters over Europe.

But it is not only Keith's story – it also belongs to a young Dutch woman named Jannie.

For what is less known about 460 Squadron is that in addition to carrying out vital bombing raids, from 29 April until 8 May 1945 the squadron also took part in Operation Manna, dropping food supplies to starving civilians in parts of Western Holland. Keith and his crew, haunted by the many bombing raids they had carried out, were overjoyed at being able to deliver hope rather than cause destruction. Keith was so elated he included his name and address with one of the parcels in the hope he would one day know who he was helping. Jannie was one of the grateful recipients and wrote Keith to express her thanks. So began a friendship that would last a lifetime.

In *The Flying Grocer* Rupert has done a magnificent job in sharing with us the intertwining stories of Keith and Jannie and their experience of the war. He shows us with notable empathy both the immense joy and the immense despair that war can bring. He also shows us the incredibly deep bond that can be forged between two people even when their contact is fleeting. Rupert's thorough research and narrative history take us back to a time when a world at peace was a distant memory and when survival was often dependent on nothing more than luck. *The Flying Grocer* is an engrossing tale of disappointment and uncertainty, of struggle and loss. Equally, though, it is a story of strength, resistance, commitment, and, above all, compassion.

As is typical for Second World War veterans, Keith Bennett was a very private man and didn't like to talk much of his time at war. In fact, I know Rupert set about writing this book weighed down with uncertainty as to whether Keith would have approved. However, after reading *The Flying Grocer* I commend Rupert for his commitment to honouring his father-in-law and his great achievements. For as the experience of war continues to recede from national memory, it is our duty to ensure the service and sacrifice of our veterans is known and remembered. This is a lasting debt we owe to all those who served our nation in uniform. And with this book it is a debt Rupert has repaid in full to Flying Officer Keith Bennett, DFC.

I am sure Keith would have thoroughly enjoyed *The Flying Grocer*, just as I did.

Air Chief Marshal Angus Houston, AO, AFC
Chief of the Defence Force (Australia)
June 2007

Introduction

'It was a very special day ... a very happy memory.'
Jannie Verstigen

IT IS LATE AFTERNOON ON 29 April 2006. Jannie Verstigen looks over her right shoulder and sees a six-lane highway flowing with a constant stream of cars and trucks. Sixty-one years ago, the view from this viaduct outside the small Dutch town of Ridderkerk and northwest towards Rotterdam showed a two-lane country road for horse-drawn carts and bikes that once dissected acres of open farm fields. Now the fields are filled with houses.

But in her mind's eye Jannie retains the image of a swarm of black low-flying Avro Lancaster bombers making their return journey to England from Rotterdam. The image is as clear to her now as an 82-year-old as it was on 1 May 1945 when, as a young woman, her world had been torn apart by war and a five-year German occupation that had plundered and pillaged her country.

Jannie's vivid recollection of 1 May 1945 is a memory she

shares with most Dutch survivors of World War II. For that was the day when the Allied bombers flew over western Holland – much as they had been doing since the outbreak of the war – only this time they were armed not with bombs but with food, medical supplies and resources. The Lancasters had come to save an estimated 3.5 million Dutch who'd been battling starvation and fighting for survival.

The Germans had occupied the region on 10 May 1940. By April 1945, however, they were facing inevitable defeat. As a parting shot, the German army sapped the region of all its food and energy resources, and flooded what was left of it by blowing up its network of canals. The humanitarian fly-by on 1 May 1945 was the result of a truce between the Allies and the occupying Germans. It was one sortie of a ten-day mission that Bomber Command named Operation Manna, soon to be complemented by Operation Chowhound when the US Air Force joined in.

Despite being one of the greatest humanitarian feats in the history of modern war, in the years that followed it went largely unrecognised, except in Holland where it is commemorated with two minutes' silence on 1 May every year.

But Jannie doesn't need commemorations to remind her of the day and the happiness it brought. 'I was in a house over there,' she says, pointing to her left and back towards the village of Ridderkerk. 'I was having typing lessons with my friend Bouwine. We heard the aeroplanes. We knew they had dropped food parcels over Rotterdam. We were so excited and ran from the house to the viaduct.'

Bouwine Van Vliet had been living with Jannie in Ridderkerk because her own family in Rotterdam had run out of food. As the two women ran to join the growing throng cheering the Lancasters, they were thinking only of relieving the hunger that had formed a constant knot in their stomachs. The long-term implications – of liberation and an end to the terror of occupation – were not front of mind. But perhaps even further from Jannie's thoughts was the notion that this food-drop would result in a life-long friendship with an Australian pilot who was flying one of the Lancasters.

As the girls approached the scene of the drop, one of the Lancasters flew so low that Jannie could see the faces of the crew. After dropping its parcel, the plane dipped its wings in the traditional airmen's signal and flew back across the Channel to Binbrook in Lincolnshire, England, from whence it had come.

The parcel contained twenty packets of cigarettes and the addresses of two of its seven-man crew: Flying Officer Keith Bennett, who was the pilot, and bomb-aimer Alby Murray. The two airmen were near the end of their tour of 30 operations. And, like the many who had risked their lives daily by dropping bombs over Germany and central Europe, they were as excited as Jannie to be ending their war performing a humanitarian mission.

Jannie recalls: 'We went to the spot where the parcel had fallen. Bouwine got hold of one packet of cigarettes. I found the address of the pilot. I wrote it down. We screamed, were excited and waving and dancing with joy.'

The war ended a week later, on 8 May 1945. Jannie and

Bouwine wrote to the Australian airmen and Jannie got a reply. 'I got a letter back from Keith Bennett and I was very proud that an Australian had written me a letter. You know how girls are at that age.' The two continued writing to each other until about 1949, when Jannie went to England for a year. Then in 1983, Keith wrote to Jannie asking if he and his wife Elva could come and visit Jannie in Holland. The letter came to Jannie via a niece as she had moved to Laren (near Amsterdam) and married.

Jannie remembers their reunion: 'It was a very nice meeting. I was nervous. It was a very happy day for me and my husband. Very nice.'

Today, Jannie often returns to the viaduct where the name Keith Bennett wafted into her life on a piece of scrap paper. 'I always think about it,' says Jannie, smiling. 'It was a very special day . . . a very happy memory.'

YEAR		AIRCRAFT		Pilot, or	2nd Pilot, Pupil	DUTY
Month	Date	Type	No.	1st Pilot	or Passenger	(Including Results and Remarks)
—	—	—	—	—	—	— Totals Brought Forward
MAY	3	LANCASTER III	G₂	SELF	F/O EMERSON	30TH. OPERATION
					SGT ENTWISTLE	SUPPLY DROPPING NEAR
					F/S MURRAY	ROTTERDAM. 4 BLOCKS
					T/S FORD	OF 284 SACKS. 416 MLS
					F/S FREEZER	WEATHER STILL. VERY
					F/S FIRKINS	SQUALLY

7. Lawrence S/L
O.C. "C" FLIGHT

W/C.
C.O. 460 SQUADRON.

SUMMARY FOR. MAY.   TYPES.
UNIT   460 SQUADRON   LANCASTER I
DATE   5·5·45   LANCASTER III.
SIGNATURE

TOTAL HOURS FOR 460 SQUADRON.

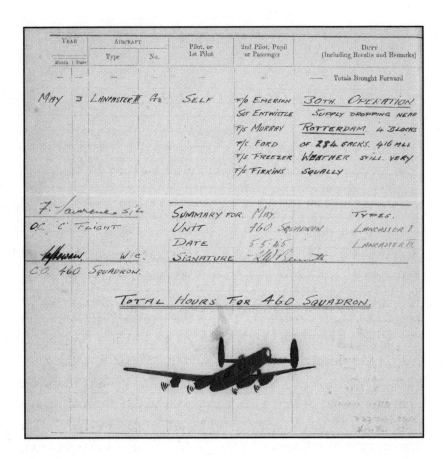

Chapter 1

Born to Fly

*Remember, always keep your 'flying speed' up,
especially near the ground.*

William George Bennett, 1944

AS THE SON OF A WORLD WAR I PILOT, flying was in Keith William
Bennett's blood. Born on 9 September 1923, he was the eldest
of four brothers. With the exception of his brother Alan, who
was too young to serve, the three other boys – Keith, Jack and
Frank – enlisted in the armed forces in World War II. Frank was
still in the Air Training Corps when the war ended, but both
Keith and Jack saw action in the Royal Australian Air Force,
albeit in vastly different circumstances. Keith enlisted at age
nineteen and went on to serve as an officer and pilot of a
Lancaster heavy bomber in the RAAF's famed 460 Squadron,
which was based in Binbrook, England, and played such a
huge role in the Allied bombings of Germany. His younger
brother Jack, who signed up at age eighteen, flew Kittyhawk

1

fighter planes with 77 Squadron and fought in the Pacific and Borneo.

The boys' father, William George Bennett, was born in the parish of Edgbaston, in Birmingham, England. An orphan raised by his aunt, he later trained as a fitter and turner. On 18 June 1914, at the age of twenty-two, Bennett snr enlisted with the Royal Flying Corps (RFC) which was then the overland air arm of the British military. In April 1918, the RFC was amalgamated with the Royal Naval Air Services and the newly combined force became known as the Royal Air Force, which it still is today.

Bennett snr's services career began as a fitter but by 1 November 1916 he had been elevated to pilot first class. By the time of his demobilisation after the war to the RAF Reserve on 2 April 1919, he had become a flight sergeant pilot who, according to his Certificate of Employment during the war, accrued 300 hours of flying time in 'about fifteen types of machines' – and not without his share of drama in the skies over France. During one operation, Bennett snr was shot through the leg from underneath. Miraculously, the bullet passed through his leg, then exited through his chest and he survived the war. Even better, he never had cause to fire a single shot.

Following the incident, Bennett snr was sent to Northern Ireland to recuperate, but what he found there was far from peaceful. The Troubles were brewing and he was dispatched to join an armed force that was to maintain law and order. Having been on the receiving end of a few too many spits from the local Irish, Bennett snr set his sights on a new life elsewhere and planned for a move to Australia, but his role as the model for a portrait titled *The NCO Pilot, RFC*, which is still stored at the Imperial War Museum in London, ensured he was immortalised in the Old Country. The portrait of Bennett snr was part of a collection painted by one of the greatest war artists, Irishman Sir William Orpen, to honour the three armed services and it accompanies portraits of a seaman, known to be a petty officer, and an army sergeant, the latter titled as *A Grenadier Guardsman*.

William Bennett arrived in Australia on 2 December 1920. Shortly afterwards, he married Catherine Jackson, who'd followed him from England. Exactly a year later, the first of their four sons – Keith – entered the world.

As a child, Keith was like most. But he did have a stammer that would remain with him for much of his life. He and his brothers attended North Sydney Boys High School. Keith excelled at mathematics and loved sport, in particular tennis and boxing – the latter a pastime he would continue when in the RAAF and quit with an undefeated record.

Towards the end of his school days, Bennett's parents, concerned about his direction in life, took him to see a careers adviser who recommended he become a plumber. He didn't.

Bennett would always have a penchant for fixing pipework and was often to be seen with wrench in hand and head underneath a basin, tinkering, but his career – which was to be put on hold during the war – would be in engineering, which he trained for after leaving school.

Despite his stammer and the effect it had on his persona – making him self-conscious in front of people – as the eldest of four brothers, Bennett still assumed all the responsibilities that came with being the leader among his siblings. His place atop the fraternal pecking order and his naturally headstrong views on issues also often led to heated arguments with his father, both before and after the war. But it was still a tightly knit family, one that participated in many activities together, from the simple to the very bizarre, such as the day during a drought when Bennett snr and his four sons took the 'pet' sheep – which they owned for grazing on the backyard to save mowing the lawn – to the Botanical Gardens in the Sydney CBD, where grass was more plentiful. The five of them – six, with the sheep – were promptly kicked out by security guards.

Keith and his brothers also dearly loved their mother, Catherine. Although from time to time she must have asked herself how much true this love was, especially when a hammock that her sons had built for her suddenly broke when she was sleeping in it one day. While she naturally forgave them, she would never forget the incident as her children grew up to become adults. In her later life, and as if to humorously restore a little of the control she once had as a mother but was destined to lose as they led their own lives, she always jokingly blamed the fall for the pain she felt with a lingering spinal condition.

When the war broke out, Keith was keen to enlist but feared he might be stopped in his tracks. His father owned a screw-manufacturing company in Sydney, which on 13 May 1940 he officially registered as W.G. Bennett and Son. Because the firm was considered to be an essential service, Keith was worried that his father might stop him from enlisting so he could work for the family firm instead, and thereby avoid the war. That his mother was also displeased about his ambitions to enlist did not help his cause. But Keith remained determined to serve, and until he could do so, he and a schoolmate, Ken Williams, chose to pass the time by joining the local militia Light Horse regiment based at Greta, near Cessnock in the Hunter Valley. Working with horses, Keith would discover, was not his forte. One night when he and Williams were assigned to look after the horses, a stampede broke out when a noise spooked them. In turn, the incident spooked Bennett, who would never touch a horse again until his late sixties when, while at Goulburn in New South Wales to look at a racehorse he was considering buying a share in, he patted it.

Throughout his time with the Light Horse regiment, he remained anxious that his path to the airforce would be blocked. His diary entry for 27 May 1942 reads: 'Hope the opportunities for getting in the Air Force will increase. Dad does not think so. Hope he will release me soon.' On 2 June 1942, he wrote: 'Dad received a letter from the Ministry of Munitions about the shortage of automatic screws. Hope it will not stop me from joining the Air Force – don't know whether he wants me to or not.' Then the next day, a more determined Keith, who was clearly intent on getting himself into top physical condition for what awaited him in Europe, penned this entry: 'A very wet day with driving rain. Must try harder to get fit. Britain sends another 1000 bombers over Essen, Germany. Hope they don't knock them out before I have a chance.'

The threat of the war coming to Australia, and a possible conflict with Japan, was another factor that had to be considered. While the war had previously centred on the Pacific, by 1942, after the fall of Singapore, it had reached Australian shores. On 19 February Darwin was bombed, followed by bomb-raids in Broome and Wyndham and, in May 1942, the sinking of Japanese midget submarines in Sydney Harbour.

It was a threat that Australia took seriously and one of which Bennett was reminded on the morning of 8 June 1942 when he was suddenly awoken with ear-piercing sirens and his father hauling him out of bed to get ready for an air-raid drill. That day he wrote in his diary: 'Had only been asleep a short while when father comes around pulling us out of bed at about 27 to 1 saying there was an air raid on. The sirens were going up [and] down full blast as we groped around looking for the blackout blinds, torches, matches etc. Then at last with the blackout blinds up we switched the lights on and the all clear signal went from a siren some distance away . . . but the local siren didn't go till about 1:10.'

Keith's youngest brother Alan remembers the air-raid drills, and how one day he found a 'practice bomb' on the bedroom dresser in his room. To this day, he is still not sure how it got there, nor what purpose it was meant to serve. But it shows how entrenched the subject of war had become in their household.

Judging by his diary entries, the air-raid drills only heightened Keith's desire to enlist. 'Hoped to have Air Force application today. Who knows when I will,' he wrote on

Saturday 13 June. Then on Monday 15 June, Keith sensed a breakthrough: 'Dad seems to have given in to this idea of me joining now and I hope to be in soon.'

Keith's wish came true, but the sudden change in fortune also alerted him to improve on one weakness that could have potentially devastating consequences in the air – his stutter. On 20 June 1942, he wrote: 'At last handed my application in for air crew at Woolloomooloo this morning. Told it would take about three weeks before I am called up for the medical. Hope it will be sooner. Must now work hard on my speech.'

As the days, then weeks, passed with no news of when he would be called up for a medical, Keith continued to study – geometry, mathematics, and drawing – and to prepare himself physically by running, skipping, doing a series of exercises he called his 'daily dozen', and playing tennis with friends and family. And as he had already been doing for months, Keith continued to take a cold shower first thing in the morning, no matter how bitter the weather. He also pondered joining the navy instead: 'Am seriously thinking about applying for the Navy to be trained as a mid-shipman or sub-lieutenant. Anyhow, I will make inquiries about it this week' he penned in his diary on Monday 6 July.

July passed into August and still his application was not approved. The need to submit a new form was looking likely, with Keith growing increasingly pessimistic about his future in the Air Force: 'Don't know what to think of my chances now of joining the Air Force. Dad says he will write a letter to accompany the second application, but I don't know if it will be any good unless I could see Squadron Leader Himmel in charge of Woolloomooloo', reads his diary on Thursday 13 August.

As it turned out, Keith had no cause to be concerned. He did get called up for a medical test and he passed. And on 8 September at Woolloomooloo, one day before his twentieth birthday, he was sworn in for the Air Training Corps and sent off to Bradfield Park, near Lindfield in Sydney's north shore, where he and other raw recruits would be based for about a week – living in Nissen huts – until their career path to the war in Europe had been settled.

On 2 January 1943, Keith enlisted as RAAF airman 432472 'for the duration of the war and for a period of 12 months thereafter', according to his record of service. Despite his reluctance to show emotion, it was clear that William Bennett was proud of his sons when both were enlisted. Younger brother Alan remembers: 'Mum, she just went about her business quietly, but just hoping that they would both come home alive.'

One of Keith's first tasks as an enlisted member of the forces was to write a will. In his, Keith left his road bicycle and cricket bat to his youngest brother, Alan, who was ten at the time. Jack also left Alan his bike. 'I was able to sell one for the money and still keep and use one for myself,' Alan says, not explaining what happened when both brothers returned home.

With two of his sons enlisted, William Bennett returned to the armed services in an honorary capacity. From 23 March 1942 to 15 May 1946, he was assigned to the No. 2 wing of RAAF Air Training Corps where he assisted in the pre-entry training of recruits.

Bennett first took up the posting as a flight instructor, but was later promoted to Squadron Leader. This afforded him the rare pleasure of presenting flying wings to his son Jack. Shortly after the end of the war, Bennett would also get to award Keith his Distinguished Flying Cross (DFC) – an honour to both father and son.

~

For Keith and Jack Bennett, following in their father's footsteps wasn't going to be easy. William Bennett was a hard man, had a temper, and was known to show it. Similarly, he bottled up emotions and rarely spoke of his war experiences. In 1944, in a letter to Keith, which the latter received just before his twenty-first birthday while stationed at Wheaton Aston, England, Bennett snr wrote:

> I find this letter very hard to write because there is so much I want to say and I can't find the words to express it. You have always been a good son and indeed have Jack, Frank and Alan. I know you have very often thought I have been hard and perhaps unfair because I was ambitious to see you all succeed in life and become good citizens. As you know I had a rather tough spin as a boy and youth and perhaps that hardened me a little. Anyway, I don't think you are any the worse for it and if it has taught you to exercise a little self-discipline it has been worthwhile.

Correspondence between the family members continued for the duration of the war. Alan recalls receiving letters from Keith, but they were short on sentiment or detailed descriptions of his experiences. 'Occasionally Keith would write about the war, but there was only so much he could say because of the censors. His letters would be more about asking "Are you behaving yourself?" or "Are you helping your mum?"' But Jack's letters from Burma were entertaining, if not for the actual content so much as for the coded messages he would write on the envelope to indicate where he was. With the war against Japan underway, there was much secrecy about where Australian servicemen and women were actually based. 'For instance, he would try and make sure the first letter of each word spelled the location from where he was sending it,' recalls Alan.

By April 1943, Keith had begun his Empire Allied Training Scheme. He was sent to the flying town of Temora, in southwest New South Wales, for his elementary flying course. He began to live out his dream of becoming a pilot by flying a two-man single-engine DH 82.

William Bennett could well appreciate his son Keith's passion to fly. In a letter dated 20 April 1943, he asked his son:

> How do you feel in the air now? Are you still as keen as ever? As you say, the sight above a layer of clouds on a nice day is wonderful. I hope you are keeping yourself fit and exercising when possible and getting plenty of sleep. That is most important when training because there is always more nerve strain during the initial course and if

you are not in good shape you just can't do yourself justice.

Well, son, you have got what you have tried a long time for and now it's up to you and I certainly wish you every success and hope you realise all your ambitions. I will be very proud of you if you do, but even if you don't just make it I will still be proud that you tried. There is no need to rush things, you know. This is going to last a long time yet. Remember, always keep your 'flying speed' up, especially near the ground.

Year		Aircraft		Pilot, or 1st Pilot	2nd Pilot, Pupil or Passenger	Duty (Including Results and Remarks)
Month	Date	Type	No.			
---	---	---	---	---	---	---— Totals Brought Forward
May	3	LANCASTER III	G₂	SELF	F/O EMERSON	30TH OPERATION
					SGT ENTWISTLE	SUPPLY DROPPING NEAR
					F/S MURRAY	ROTTERDAM. 4 BLOCKS
					F/S FORD	OF 284 SACKS. 416 MLS
					F/S FREEZER	WEATHER STILL VERY
					F/S FIRKINS	SQUALLY

F. Lawrence S/L
O.C. 'C' FLIGHT

(signature) W/C
C.O. 460 SQUADRON.

SUMMARY FOR. MAY		TYPES.
UNIT	460 SQUADRON	LANCASTER I
DATE	5.5.45	LANCASTER III.
SIGNATURE	_(signature)_	

TOTAL HOURS FOR 460 SQUADRON.

Chapter 2

The Bridge is Down

*The Germans . . . always had these bloody black boots
on. There was this tremendous noise: 'click clack,
click clack'. You could hear them from miles away.*

Henk Benness

JANNIE VAN SPLUNDER WAS SUDDENLY AWOKEN at 4 am by the thunderous roar of planes – German Junker 88s and Messerschmitt 109s and 110s – as they flew high in the skies and across the harbour town of Ridderkerk, southeast of Amsterdam. Curious as much as she was afraid, she rushed from her bed in the attic room to look out the window and follow their flight path. The noise, combined with the sinister silhouettes of Luftwaffe planes against the faint pre-dawn light, were the tell-tale signs of a German invasion. It was 10 May 1940.

The Dutch should have been better prepared. Agents of the Dutch military ensconced in Berlin had forewarned of a German attack the day before. But all such previous warnings had always been false alarms. Hence, when their latest alert – *Morgen vroeg bij het krieken van de dag. Houdt stand!* (Tomorrow morning at dawn. Hold fast!) – came through, it was not heeded either.

For Jannie Van Splunder and her fellow Dutch, the price of that complacency would be high indeed. Life as she knew it would not be the same again for a long time. Within minutes, what appeared to be thousands of German troops were parachuting out of the planes and onto Dutch soil. One battalion landed at the airfield at Waalhaven, south of Rotterdam. Another battalion of paratroopers landed about 16 kilometres further southeast in Dordrecht, with the objective to take over the bridge in the centre of town and thus enable access for the impending arrival of German land forces and vehicles. Dutch defences were rapidly tested in the town of Maastricht further south of Ridderkerk; then to the north at The Hague where Queen Wilhelmina and the Dutch Royal family and the Dutch government were based; followed by defences at Ypenburg, Valkenburg and Ockenburg.

Jannie monitored the progress of the war by checking the Noord River Bridge. Having seen the arrival of the German planes, every day she'd run up to the attic, peer out its small window and look east towards the river, hoping to see the steel-arched bridge still up – signalling that the Germans had not yet arrived at Ridderkerk. Once it was down, she knew that her town's fears of German occupation would become a frightening reality. When Jannie checked the bridge on 12 May, she found to her horror that it was down.

Dutch defences were horribly ill-equipped to deal with the

invading Germans. While they had bolstered their army following the rise of Adolf Hitler in Germany, they did so at a rate far slower than the other European powers, who were quick to suspect Hitler's aims. The Dutch army's lack of resources spelled nothing short of disaster for the impending Battle of the Netherlands. To fend off a German invasion force numbering 22 divisions, 1378 guns, 759 tanks, 1150 aircraft (including then relatively modern Stuka dive-bombers) and 750,000 men armed with sub-machine guns, the Dutch had 9 divisions, 676 howitzers and field guns, one non-operational tank, 155 aircraft (75 of them biplanes) and 350,000 men, most of whom were poorly trained and armed only with the outdated pre-World War I Steyr-Mannlicher M1895 bolt-action rifles.

Miraculously, by the morning of 13 May, the Dutch were still fending off the Germans as they held the north bank of the Nieuwe Maas River that runs through the centre of Rotterdam. By then Queen Wilhelmina and her government had already moved to England, where they would live out the war in London, leaving official authority – or what remained of it – with General H.G Winkelman, the commander-in-chief of the defiant Dutch army. But it would be a short-lived authority, for, livid that his forces had not made short shrift of the invasion, Hitler ordered the bombing of Dutch cities, starting with Rotterdam, to force their surrender. Plans were in place for the attack, but German land forces that were holding the south bank of the river made a final attempt to negotiate with the Dutch for a non-aggressive surrender.

Yet just as the Dutch negotiator was walking back across the

Willemsburg Bridge to tell his superiors that negotiations were successful and that the impending attack had been forestalled, all hell suddenly broke loose.

At 13.20, the skies above the Netherlands became pock-marked with 90 Heinkel HE111 heavy bombers from KG54 Squadron that were swarming towards Rotterdam. And as they came over the Dutch port city, 57 of them dropped their full load over the city. The final toll was an estimated 800–900 deaths, 70,000 homeless, and the levelling of 2.6 square kilometres of city that destroyed 24,978 homes, 24 churches, 2320 shops, 775 warehouses and 62 schools. The scars of those devastating raids are still evident to this day, with the old Willemsburg Bridge still not re-built, but replaced with a new one of the same name that crosses the river 100 metres to the east. At the base of the old bridge on Noodereiland, a small islet in the middle of the Nieuwe Maas River, there is a giant painted mural of the city's history which portrays the German Luftwaffe bombers dropping their massive loads onto the town.

Henk Benness, a Dutchman who was then thirteen and who today lives in Lane Cove, Sydney, remembers the raid well. From his bedroom in the town of Gouda, northeast of Ridderkerk, he'd seen the German planes fly over his family and the German paratroopers who jumped out. 'They had something like 500 paratroopers that they dropped behind the waterline, mainly near The Hague. And to make it look like a bigger force they actually threw out straw men. So they were behind the defence line. But at that time we were not very frightened of the planes. They just seemed to go over us. It was only a few days later that Rotterdam was bombed.'

Benness remembers the dogfights in the air over Rotterdam and the final arrival of the Germans invading on land – by motorbike, car, truck and foot. The latter he heard before he saw, as he recalls: 'The first Germans came in motorcars and motor-bikes. They always had these bloody black boots on, and they marched, and there was this tremendous noise: "click clack, click clack". You could hear them coming from miles away.'

The invasion immediately incited a mass exodus of Dutch civilians from the city into the country. As Benness says: 'People left their homes because of all the shooting and bombing. We saw people with their bikes loaded up with blankets and house-hold kits and they were taken in by people in towns.'

Following Germany's threat to repeat the bombing attacks on Amsterdam, Utrecht, and then The Hague, General H. G. Winkelman saw no option but to agree to an immediate sur-render on 15 May, which was signed at the town of Rijsoord.

The Battle of the Netherlands ended with 7500 Dutch sol-diers either killed, wounded or missing, and 343,500 captured. German losses amounted to 4000 deaths, 3000 wounded, 700 missing, and 1400 captured and transported as prisoners across the Channel to Britain.

But the real price was far greater. For despite initial hope that the Allies would resolve the hostilities by quickly pushing back the Germans, the battle led to five years of occupation that would see hundreds of thousands of people die by execution, bombing raids, or starvation.

The bombing of Rotterdam also had serious consequences

for the war at large. For until then, Great Britain and France had pledged to agree to US President Franklin D. Roosevelt's plea that all warring parties in Europe limit their bombing raids to military targets. The Allies' agreement was conditional upon Germany abiding by the same terms. With the bombing of Rotterdam, however, Germany contravened this condition. Hence, Britain and France were pushed to throw humanitarian terms out the door.

On 15 May, the RAF was granted permission to bomb the Ruhr, targeting oil plants and any industrial target that aided the German war effort, even if it contained a civilian population. That night, the RAF carried out its first raid inside Germany – the first of thousands of such operations.

All across Holland, the Dutch were placed under strict orders. At night, blackouts and curfews were enforced. This was as much an attempt to disorientate Allied bombing forces that were constantly flying over Holland to bomb Germany as it was to protect the town from bomb attacks, as Germany used the region's port networks to transport supplies, troops and armaments to and from its occupied territories.

Jannie remembers how the German troops set up camps wherever they felt like it. The front garden of her family home was quickly seized upon by German units, so too were any spare bedrooms in their house where she lived with her twin sisters, Rookje and Wilhelmina; her mother, Wilhelmina; and her father. 'There was a harbour in Ridderkerk for small ships.

The Germans set up camp there, and stayed there for years. My parents always had German officers in their house.'

But as the Germans took over Ridderkerk – known for its shipyards and engineering works as much as for its produce-farming – the town's inhabitants had no idea that the occupation would last five years. At that stage, they could not have imagined the extent of the devastation that would result from German rule: the starvation, illness, and for all too many, their deaths.

During the initial stages of the invasion, the Germans offered the Dutch government the chance of collaboration, similar to their arrangement with the Vichy government in France. Yet the Dutch refused, electing instead to maintain their exile in England. Hence, the Nazis had to put their own governing systems in place. They installed a military government headed by Arthur Seyss-Inquart, an Austrian Nazi who soon came to be feared and despised. As Henk Benness remembers, he was a man whose stature and authority belied his actual appearance. 'He was a funny sort of bloke to watch,' says Benness, who saw him once. 'He had this enormous cap on his head, and one of his legs was shorter than the other. And sometimes when he went to look at the troops he used to walk with one leg on the pavement and the other one in the gutter. It was quite funny, but he was a bit of a bastard.'

The government policy was termed *Gleichschaltung* – in English, synchronising – which effectively meant ridding the nation of any organisation that was not aligned with the Nazis. This policy was aimed not only at the Jews, but also at the socialists, liberals, Catholics and Protestants, among others. The Germans also attempted to enact a sweeping national-socialist policy in the Netherlands; but despite the success of this movement before the war in the form of the National Socialistische Beweging (NSB; National Socialist Movement), the poor state of the Dutch economy meant it didn't work following the invasion.

Shortly after their arrival, the Germans installed authoritarian rule. They were helped by a considerable number of Dutch collaborators – the NSB especially, whose 100,000 membership included about 3 per cent of the Dutch male population in 1941, came to the fore. Indeed, the NSB played a major role in controlling the lower government and civil service, and every town mayor appointed by the Germans was an NSB member. The NSB was disbanded after the war, and while some members were arrested and charged, most escaped retribution.

However, Dutch collaboration was not only centred on internal operations of government. Between 20,000 and 25,000 Dutchmen enlisted in the German armed forces. They fought in specially set up Dutch brigades called the Heer and the Waffen-SS. The most noted of these brigades was the 4th SS Volunteer Panzergrenadier Brigade Nederland which fought on the Eastern Front. Indeed, some Dutch recruits even distinguished themselves – such as in the Battle of Narva in 1944 – and a number received Nazi Germany's highest bravery award, the Knight's Cross.

In Rotterdam, the Nazi persecution of the Jews was not as widespread in the early days of occupation as it would become from 1941 on, when the city's 12,000-strong Jewish population was ultimately reduced to less than 2000 by the end of the war. Two synagogues were destroyed in the bombardment on 14 May 1940, and many Jews had already begun to flee the city. But this did not stop the Germans from enforcing new laws that inevitably led to their massacre. From September 1941, Jewish children were banned from attending normal schools and made to enrol in Jewish-only schools. Then from May 1942, all Jews were forced to wear the yellow Star of David and carry identity cards stamped with a large capital 'J'. Placards reading 'Jews not allowed' were placed at the entrances of public facilities like parks, pubs, cinemas, theatres and sporting grounds. Then on 30 July, the Nazis assigned 'Shed 24' – a shed on Rotterdam Port – as a rallying point where Jews were ordered to gather before being deported to camps throughout the German-occupied territories.

Despite the new authoritarian order, one thing that was not missing during the early years of German occupation was food and resources. Food coupons, or *bonnen*, could be exchanged for food supplies – depending of course on availability, and that the coded numbers printed on them correlated with the numbers alongside the list of available foods that were published in Saturday's newspaper.

The newspaper was not just a tool for the Dutch to get food; the Germans used it to push government propaganda. Headlines on posters plastered throughout the country and in newspapers such as the *Volk en Vaderland*, which was run by the NSB, read: 'With Germany against capitalism',

'Germany triumphs for Europe on all fronts', or 'V' for victory.

But despite the existence of the NSB, the Dutch did not sit back and live under German rule without a fight. Before too long, a Dutch Resistance was formed, if only as an unofficial force initially, enacting small acts of rebellion – such as turning the letter 'V' for victory, which the Germans proclaimed on billboards and placards, into a W for Queen Wilhelmina. For despite the severity of German rule, and the eventual pillaging of Dutch food and resources, the Nazis could not stymie the Dutch fighting spirit.

YEAR		AIRCRAFT		Pilot, or 1st Pilot	2nd Pilot, Pupil or Passenger	DUTY (Including Results and Remarks)
Month	Date	Type	No.			
—	—	—	—	—		—— Totals Brought Forward
MAY	3	LANCASTER III	G2	SELF	F/O EMERSON	30TH. OPERATION
					Sgt ENTWISTLE	SUPPLY DROPPING NEAR
					F/S MURRAY	ROTTERDAM. 4 BLOCKS
					T/S FORD	OF 284 SACKS. 416 MLS
					T/S FREEZER	WEATHER STILL VERY
					F/S FIRKINS	SQUALLY

F. Lawrence S/L
O.C. 'C' FLIGHT

SUMMARY FOR. MAY.   TYPES.
UNIT   460 SQUADRON   LANCASTER I
DATE   5.5.45   LANCASTER III
SIGNATURE   RW Bennett

—— W/C.
C.O. 460 SQUADRON.

TOTAL HOURS FOR 460 SQUADRON.

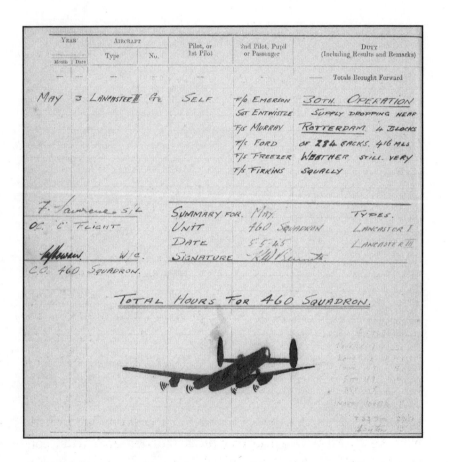

Chapter 3

Ready or Not

Q: So what attracted the others to Bennett as a pilot?
A: It was simple. We needed a pilot, didn't we? We
would have been pretty bloody useless without one.

Alby Murray

On 26 April 1943, six days after receiving the touching letter from his father, Keith Bennett, now Leading Aircraftman and with nineteen flights to his name, took off from Temora at the start of his fifty-week course to become a pilot, and for his first solo sortie. He was travelling in a two-seater two-blade propeller De Havilland 82 Tiger Moth (DH 82).

To ensure correct weight distribution and balance on this solo flight, Bennett had to sit in the rear cockpit, like he'd do were he flying with an instructor. A wooden and metal constructed light biplane, the DH 82 evolved from the popular Gypsy Moth used during World War I. But by the time World War II came around, it was regarded as the ideal plane for basic pilot training. It had a wingspan of 8.4 metres, was 2.9 metres long, 2.70 metres high, with a maximum speed of 175 km/h, a range of 459 km, a climbing ability of 205 m/minute, a ceiling height capacity of 4145 metres and weighed 506 kg when empty and 828 kg when fully loaded.

Within a month, Bennett had flown the DH 82 solo another 22 times and had accrued 60 hours of flying time from a total of 71 flights during both day and night sorties. His flight log containing the 31 May report-card announced that he'd reached 'required standard' as a pilot. But by the following month, he was ready to try his hand flying another single-engine plane: the Wirraway in Uranquinty.

More than 1500 RAAF recruits graduated from the Service Flying Training School at Uranquinty, a small rural town south of Temora in the Riverina district of southwestern New South Wales. And while the base has since been abandoned, its remains now on a private property, a memorial of an old Wirraway engine still stands in the town centre in honour of those RAAF airmen who lost their lives in the war, especially those among them who were not identified.

Bennett trained at Uranquinty from 9 June to 9 August 1943. In doing so, he added cross-country map-reading and flying at low level and at night to his increasing arsenal of pilot skills. By the time he was ready to leave, his flying time was 118 hours and 30 minutes.

The Wirraway – an Aboriginal word for 'challenge' – was a two-seater general purpose monoplane that derived from the North American NA-33. It was commissioned by Wing

Commander Sir Lawrence Wackett in 1936, and made its first delivery to the RAAF as the A20-1 and A20-2 in July 1939. The Wirraway was powered by one 600 hp Wasp nine-cylinder air-cooled radial engine and made with an all-metal stressed coating. It had a 13.10 metre wingspan, 8.48 metre length and 2.66 metre height, and was twice as fast as the Tiger Moth with its maximum speed of 354 km/h. Its superiority extended to other areas too. Its maximum range was 1158 km, it had a climbing ability of 594 m/minute, ceiling capacity of 7010 metres and weighed 1811 kg when empty and 2991 kg when fully loaded. It also came with two synchronised .303 guns above the fuselage, a rear manual-operated .303 gun, and could carry a light bomb-load beneath its wings. But while the Wirraway was deployed to Malaya, Darwin and Rabaul and sporadically used in action, it was too slow a plane to make a real impact in battle.

Bennett's step up to the Wirraway from the DH 82 was not easy. His instructor's report, dated 5 August, said that although he'd reached 'required standard', his 'night flying was inconsistent'. Nevertheless, Bennett commenced advanced training five days later and was again in the Wirraway at Uranquinty, where he remained for another six weeks.

Despite a little further criticism – his instructor's log report for 23 September said 'aerobatics weak' – Bennett still passed, officially becoming an airman pilot.

His training continued – from Pre-Advanced Flying Unit classes in January–March 1944 where he again flew DH 82s and was promoted to Flight Sergeant, to England where he joined the AFU in April at the small military aerodrome north of

Wheaton Aston, a village 15 km southwest of Stafford in Staffordshire. There Bennett flew the twin-engine Airspeed Oxford, as he would again in June in the Beam Approach Training program at the Central Navigation School in Shawbury, Shropshire, when his flying time mounted to 287 hours 35 minutes.

The Oxford stemmed from the Airspeed eight-seater commercial plane and prepared Bennett for flying with a crew – a navigator, radio operator and gunner. Apart from being used as a training craft, the Oxford was also deployed into the services to work on anti-submarine missions, and as an ambulance in the Middle East. It was operated by two Armstrong Siddeley Cheetah X radial engines that ran at 355 hp each, had a maximum speed of 185 mph (298 km/h) at 2500 metres, range of 1500 km, ceiling height of 5850 metres, climbing rate of 4.8 m/second and had a .303 Vickers K machine gun in the dorsal turret to protect itself. It could also carry 110 kg of bombs externally.

After the war, the Oxford was re-converted to a commercial plane, but as a six-seater known as the AS65 Consul. It was not an easy plane to fly, even in training.

It was fitted with fixed pitch Fairey-Reed propellers, but a pitch lever was still located in the cockpit for the pilot to become accustomed to switching from 'coarse' to 'fine' when landing – an act that would prepare him for doing so in bombers later on.

It also had a tendency to 'yaw' (or tip to one side) that made many a landing difficult. But none of this stopped Bennett from qualifying for bomber training – which he began in England in

July 1944 in the pilot seat of a Wellington.

For his big bomber training, Bennett joined the 27 Operational Training Unit (OTU) at Lichfield. It was here that Bennett, then a provisional captain, was first crewed with another five airmen – the seventh did not join them until after he and his crew had begun flying Lancasters. It's interesting that despite so much being invested in every airman – and that their lives depended on each man's capability – the formation of a crew was a bizarrely ad-hoc affair. Everyone in the OTU was corralled into a giant hall and then ordered by the commanding officer to 'crew up' – that is, to sort themselves into crews before the CO returned. Considering that the airmen before him had come from various backgrounds and training locations – from as far afield as the United States and Canada – and knew little of each other, one could view this as the biggest and riskiest decision many of them would make in their wartime flying careers.

Records show that Bennett and his crew – all of whom survived the war – chose well; especially as statistics showed that only one in five airmen who flew on Lancasters at Bomber Command would survive. Three of the men who found themselves under Bennett's command by the time the commanding officer returned were 'scrubbed' pilots – airmen who had enlisted hoping to become pilots, but were deemed better suited for other positions.

Alby Murray was the crew's bomb-aimer. A twenty-year-old furniture-maker from Maitland, New South Wales, who came to the RAF from the army, Murray began his EFTS course at Temora and Uranquinty, but he had never met Bennett.

Like Bennett, he'd hoped to become a pilot but he was scrubbed and sent to North America to train up. Murray had the best view in the plane from the 'blister' nodule from which he would look down onto the bombing targets below. These blisters also had an upward capsule for the firing of two Browning 303 guns. While lining up to bomb their targets, bomb-aimers would be in the prone position. To their right was a panel with an array of switches and dials. Included among them were sixteen bomb selector switches, below which was a device for stick bombing and a dial with which the bomb-aimer would be able to set the timing interval between each bomb. The order of dropping bombs from the 10-metre-long bomb bay was also vital as it would help keep the Lancaster balanced. Other switches were for a camera and photo-flare, a slip heater for the 1814 kg bomb or 'cookie' to stop it from freezing up or being 'hung up', and the bomb release button.

Bomb-aimers were meant to be in their capsule only between take-offs and landings. However, many took up their positions in those moments because of the difficulty of moving from one position to the other with their parachute harnesses on. When bombs were being dropped, the only crew who spoke were the bomb-aimer and captain, the latter receiving directional instructions such as 'more left, left . . . right' to pinpoint the accuracy of a drop until he would announce: 'bombs away, skip'.

The crew's wireless operator was Harold 'Henry' Ford, a twenty-year-old teacher from the Mornington Peninsula, Victoria. He'd also been in the army before enlisting with the

RAAF. He was sent to Western Australia to join the ambulance unit as a motorbike dispatch rider where he was based at Geraldton and Miunginui. Ford wanted to be a pilot but 'mucked up [his] coordination test' and thus chose to become a wireless operator, a position that saw him first transferred to Ballarat to fly Wacketts for specific training for six months and then to Sale for gunnery training where they flew on Fairey Battles. In time, Ford received his sergeant's stripes and was formally classified as a wire air gunner before being given two weeks' leave and then posted to Sydney to await orders. He was shipped out on the *Mount Vernon* to the United States, then to the war in Europe on a ship that carried about 17,000 American troops and 70 air crew.

As the radio operator – also known as the w/op or 'sparks' – Ford found himself in the warmest place in the Lancaster because it was located next to the warm air outlet. Apart from operating the Lancaster's radio, his duties also required that he was au fait with the navigator's equipment, the plane's electrical and intercom systems, as well as be equipped to provide first-aid to any crew member injured or hurt. And when under attack by the Luftwaffe night-fighters, he would often act as an extra set of eyes for the rear and mid-upper gunners, providing alerts for impending attacks. A further task was to be on call to check for bomb 'hang ups' in the bomb bay and the flare chute from which photographic flare and 'window' – silver alfoil strips that would help Lancasters to slip through the enemy's radar unnoticed – were released.

The crew's navigator was Les Emmerson, a 32-year-old

teacher from Perth, Western Australia. While also a scrubbed pilot, Emmerson was already a commissioned officer and held rank over Bennett when he first crewed up at Lichfield, though this changed as Bennett was soon commissioned and made captain.

As the crew's navigator, Emmerson would rarely leave his position, so busy was he from the moment of the crew's take-off to when it returned to base. His work station was an array of pencils, maps and navigational tools. While in service, Emmerson did leave his position once – when 'invited' by his crew to take a glimpse at the flak during a bombing raid over Germany. He lasted barely a few seconds before he rushed back to his post, pulled back the curtain and said, 'I'll never do that again.'

Peter Firkins was the rear-tail gunner. At age eighteen, he was the youngest in the crew; he'd just left school when he volunteered for service at the RAAF. Born in Penang, Malaysia, he was brought up in Perth. He loved outdoor life, in particular playing tennis. As the tallest member of the crew at about 196 cm, with broad shoulders, he was the most unlikely person to be deemed suitable for the cramped conditions of the rear Frazer Nash FN20 turret where he also commanded two 303 Browning machine guns. But the position – known as a 'tail-end Charlie' and regarded as one of the most dangerous – was one that he accepted and held with distinction.

As a rear-tail gunner, Firkins' position was also the loneliest in the crew. As soon as they boarded, he would turn left while the others went right. His only contact with the other crew members was by intercom. To make things even tougher, the position was the most uncomfortable – although some begged to differ when compared to the mid-upper gunner. The major inconvenience for rear-gunners was leg space in the Fraser Nash FN20 turret – and in Firkins' case this was an understatement, considering his height. On many operations, Firkins would not bother to close the sliding doors behind him, preferring to sit on the frame of the entrance for extra leg space.

The crew's mid-upper gunner was Alex Freezer. A married sheep station manager with two children from rural Western Australia, Freezer was the oldest in the crew. Although he never gave his age away, he was nicknamed 'Granddad'; they guessed he was in his mid-thirties.

Freezer's position was also uncomfortable, but for different reasons than his counterpart in the rear turret. At least he got to sit on a canvas sling, his head and shoulders protruding into the Perspex dome that was on top of the fuselage, giving him a 360-degree perspective to watch for attacking night-fighters and fire his two guns. However, he was not protected from the biting draught that would blow beneath his groin region and through the inside of the Lancaster; this would often prove to be near-unbearable. Another and more notable hazard was that the mid-upper gunner was arguably in the most vulnerable position of all. Not only did he have no armoured protection – as was the case with all in the crew, bar the pilot whose seat and headrest were armoured – his turret in the middle of the plane acted like a target for German fighter planes.

What brought them all together was more a mixture of

intuition and chance than any natural gift of insight into each other's capability. The process began with segments of crews forming first. At one end of the room, Murray and Emmerson – who had shared expertise in navigation and map-reading due their similar training – saw merit in teaming up. Then, as Murray remembers, 'We found two gunners [in Firkins and Freezer]' which made four. Meanwhile, Ford had volunteered to crew with Bennett. He'd initially approached another pilot who looked older and more experienced than the others but he was rejected. 'I was a bit deflated at that,' he remembers, and decided to opt out rather than approach someone else and 'make a fool of [himself]'. But suddenly, he looked up and standing before him was Bennett and his new crewmates. It was a simple decision to join them. 'They said, "We've crewed up. How would you like to fly with us?" I said, "Goodo, thanks for approaching me."'

So what attracted the other four to Bennett as a pilot? 'It was simple. We needed a pilot didn't we? We would have been pretty bloody useless without one,' remarked Murray.

The final and seventh crew member joined them at Lancaster Flying School in Sandtoft.

Cyril Entwistle, the sole Englishman in the crew, became their flight engineer. A toolmaker and policeman's son from a village near Skipton in Yorkshire, Entwistle was first posted to Cardington in Bedford where he became a member of the guard signals or 'Dad's Army'. There it was suggested that his military vocation was as a flight engineer, as he recalls: 'This bloke said, "What about [being] an engineer?" I said, "I haven't got a clue about that." "Oh, we'll teach you," he said. "You don't need to worry about that, we'll soon hammer it into you."'

In Bomber Command, there was a shortfall of Australians who'd been trained to be flight engineers, hence their choice of an Englishman. But despite 460 Squadron being Australian, Entwistle's different nationality was no obstacle. He remembers his first meeting with Bennett: 'We just chatted and got on.' Bennett's experience in Halifaxes and Wellingtons also helped. 'I did all my flight training on Lancasters, then we went to Halifaxes. It was a different fuel system, everything was different in the Halifax to what I'd been taught on the Lancaster,' said Entwistle. 'And when we started flying, Keith had already done things like spins and stall . . . It was just a matter of getting a feel of it.'

But as an Englishman, he admitted to having had a few reservations about joining an otherwise all-Australian crew. 'I was absolutely glad to be with Australians. But I was a bit apprehensive in as much as the Australians had quite a reputation from the First World War and you think: "Oh my God, am I going to live up to their expectations?"'

As the flight engineer, Entwistle was one of the most important crew for Bennett. He had to know the Lancaster like the back of his hand, as much if not more so than the pilot and the wireless operator; basically he had to be a Jack of all trades. The flight engineer also had to be a pragmatist: a man who could think calmly under pressure, and be able to communicate as clearly and quickly as possible with his captain. Entwistle and Bennett would be in constant communication before and during operations, always checking for fuel, oil and electronic levels that – as they would discover – would prove to have lifesaving consequences.

Considering he was the last man to join the crew – and an Englishman to boot – one might expect Entwistle to have had some trouble breaking into the group. Yet he quickly became a popular and respected addition to Bennett's team. His source of information and data was a panel on his starboard (right side) that had fuel and oil gauges, fuel tank selector cocks, ammeters, booster pump switches, fuel pressure warning lights, emergency air control and oil dilution buttons. When not at his position, the flight engineer sat in a secondary 'dicky' seat to the right of the captain, providing a second set of eyes.

For Bennett, captaining a crew on top of being the pilot did not come naturally. And not only because of his stutter and the fact that privately, he often wondered how he'd made it so far. His provisional appointment as a crew captain required a lot more than having flying skills and becoming familiar with the 15-page handbook he was given that explained the qualities required for the job.

It has been said that no leader in the armed services carried as much responsibility as the captain who flew and was in charge of the Lancaster. However, his leadership was not only necessary in the air, but also on land. Hence, despite sharing the intimacy of many near-death experiences in the skies, upon the return to 'terra firma' the captain had to maintain a certain distance from his crew.

According to Bennett's handbook, the essential qualities of a captain were leadership, devotion to duty, example, service knowledge, ability to make decisions, and punctuality. He was also told that being a pilot did not automatically mean he was chosen as captain. As the handbook says:

> Your training as a pilot has covered more aspects of a bomber crew's training than any other member of your crew, and for these reasons you have provisionally been chosen to be the Captain. If during your course you are found to lack these qualifications and are unable to make a good Captain, another member of the crew more fitted to accept the responsibilities will be chosen. By virtue of these added responsibilities, and the necessity for careful selection, it is an honour to be a Captain.

The handbook goes on to list the eight responsibilities of a captain:

1. To command and lead his crew at all times both on the ground and in the air.

2. To maintain the morale of his crew and instil punctuality and obedience to all instructions on the ground and in the air.

3. To encourage his crew to keep in training and up-to-date in the own particular spheres.

4. To ensure that his crew and his aircraft are at all times in a fit state to undertake whatever task they may be called upon to perform, and to see that all parts of the aircraft are carefully checked before any flying operation, and so avoid delayed take-off or abortive sorties.

5. To maintain the standard of his aircrew's drills at the highest pitch.

6. To pass on orders of the Flight Commander to his crew and to see that they are carried out.

7. To bring to the notice of his Flight Commander all cases of devotion to duty and continued good service, and also all cases of ill discipline in his crew which he cannot correct himself, and those who appear unable to stand up to the strain of flying operations.

8. As the individual responsible for his crew he will be present on all occasions when any of his crew appears before a senior officer, on a disciplinary charge, or to receive an official commendation.

The booklet even offered Bennett and provisional captains like him advice on how to fulfil those responsibilities, the foremost tip being to take the initiative and be proactive in learning: 'As soon as you arrive at your OTU, or any unit to which you and your crew may be posted in the future, find your way and discover who's who. See where you are quartered, find out the times of duties and lectures and be in a position to guide your crew and answer all their questions. You will then have established yourself as their leader and they will begin to rely on you.'

Captains were then told about seven key points: command and leadership; maintenance of morale and discipline; training; efficiency of crew and aircraft; aircrew drills; execution of orders; and the bearing of your crew.

Command and leadership

- In order to command and lead a crew you must endeavour to convince them of your ability to cope with any emergency and to make quick and sound decisions.

- When a decision is required, think twice and then have the courage of your convictions. Do not allow yourself to be influenced by grumbles and criticisms once you have decided. This will indicate weakness and lower your prestige; then you will lose the confidence of the crew.

- If the decision calls for considerations of aspects other than those connected with actual flying, remember that each of your crew is a specialist and call on him to advise you where you need it, on his own particular task.

- Never call a conference in the air. If the airworthiness of your aircraft and its endurance are in doubt when in the air consult the engineer for airworthiness and navigator for endurance, but not the others. The air gunner is not qualified to advise you on these matters and you alone must decide.

- As a pilot you are tied to your seat the whole time while in the air; you cannot visit each member of your crew and see how they get on. Your must therefore keep your check by talking only. A few questions to each member on his own job at regular intervals will keep them up to the mark and convince them that you are in touch with the whole working of your crew and appreciate the situation at all times.

- Never let one member talk too much, or too little. An occasional rebuke will remind them who is Captain.

Maintenance of morale and discipline

- A bad Captain will produce bad morale in his crew.

- To maintain their morale you must at all times have the complete trust of your crew and their respect for your ability.

- You will soon notice a nervous member of your crew.

You must help him and encourage him. In the air you should talk to him and ask how he is getting on rather more frequently, this will keep him occupied.

- If another member is too talkative and makes observations calculated to upset a nervous man make him keep quiet.

- If you have had a sticky trip, it is up to you to 'shoot a line' afterwards and make the whole crew feel proud of themselves.

- Punctuality and strict obedience to orders will make your crew stand out among the others. They will gain credit and become more efficient, both of which tend to improve morale.

Training

- As already explained, it is impossible for Squadron and Flight Commanders to exercise detailed supervision over each individual in their squadron or flight. This applies particularly to training. If an individual is inclined to be lazy it's only his Captain who can spur him on and see that he does train.

- To fulfil this responsibility you must do two things: (a) set a high example by keeping yourself in training practice both in purely pilot matters, and also in the subjects of each member of your crew. This will give you a working knowledge of their trades and enable you to discover any weaknesses from which they suffer; (b) discover where their training is given and what their program includes. If new devices or instructions arrive, see to it that they know all about them before anyone else.

- Take and show a keen interest in the training results of each member, and where possible get them interested in each other's work.

Efficiency of crew and aircraft

- To ensure that your aircrew and aircraft always get off to time and complete the task, you must train them, to prepare for everything in good time and use methods in their checks.

- Have a check of all their flying clothing, and your own at frequent intervals whenever opportunity occurs. Always be sure that the oxygen and intercom system of your crew works. Testing apparatus for both is provided in the cloakroom. If either fails to work in the air your flight will be abortive.

- Before leaving the flights for your aircraft, check

quickly that no one has forgotten anything. Helmets and parachutes are often left behind, and sometimes the rations and colours of the day are missed because each man thought another would get them.

- When you get to the aircraft insist that each member carries out a regular and complete cockpit check, in his own position.

- Don't let your gunner mislead by saying his turret won't rotate, before the engines have started. They were never intended to, but time has often been wasted through a simple mistaken idea like that. A good Captain will know the answer straight away.

- Always give yourself and your crew more time to get out of the aircraft than they need. It is seldom that some little hitch does not occur.

- Make certain that your crew is the smartest, best trained and most efficient in your course and your squadron.

Aircrew drills

- During ground training you will be given a set number of crew drills. When you arrive in your flight, and afterwards your squadron, these drills must generally be organised by you, the Captain. Endeavour to do these drills at regular intervals, and no matter how good they be always insist that they become better and quicker.

- Regular practice in crew drills is absolutely VITAL, and one day the crew may thank you for being insistent on practising.

Execution of orders

- As has been explained, you are the link in the chain of responsibility between the Flight Commander and individual crew members.

- Make sure you understand the orders fully before you leave the Flight Commander or instructor. If you get them wrong you may make a fool of yourself in front of your crew, and in any case, waste time.

- Never allow any of them to dispute the orders, even though you may doubt the wisdom of the orders yourself. On those occasions you yourself should question them at the time they are given.

The bearing of your crew

- When in action there is no one but the members of

each crew who can report on each other's reactions under fire.

- Recognition of bravery or continued outstanding good work in difficult circumstances is of the greatest importance in maintaining the morale of all crews in the squadron. You, as Captain, will be given most of the credit for successful flights. It is your duty to see that the good efforts and actions of your crew are brought to the notice of your Flight Commander.

- In the same way, when you are unable to control any of them, or suspect they have lost their nerve, or are inefficient, you MUST tell your Flight Commander. Troublesome or useless members of crews have a very bad effect not only on their own crew, but the squadron or unit as a whole.

- On such occasions you must not let your personal feelings influence you. It is in your own interests as well as your duty to bring all these matters to the notice of those in command.

Bennett and his crew would soon find out about his ability as a pilot and captain – as each of them would about each other's qualities. The time came when they were transferred from Lichfield to the satellite base at Church Broughton, another small village in Derbyshire located about 16 kilometres southwest of Derby. The crew remained at Church Broughton, flying Vickers Wellingtons from late July to mid-September.

The Wellington was a twin-engine medium bomber that had a range of 3540 km and was affectionately known by most of those who flew it as 'Wimpy' after J. Wellington Wimpy, the friend of the cartoon character Popeye; or as 'The Flying Cigar'. Designed in the 1930s, Wellingtons were the aircraft of choice for Bomber Command in the first two years of World War II. They were extremely durable, with their geodetic lattice-work construction (steel channel beams) of the fuselage keeping the plane intact and capable of flying after being hit, despite the number and size of the holes. However, the relative slow speed of the Wellington (410 km/h max), its small bomb-load (2041 kg), and limited ceiling (6710 m) made them vulnerable and they soon fell out of favour once the Avro Lancaster was made. Not that Wellingtons were discarded for good. Sixteen models were made over the duration of the war for a total of 11,461 planes, the last of which still exists today. It is one of only two Wellingtons in the world – one of which is on display at the RAF Museum in Hendon, near London; the other, a model MK1A salvaged from the bottom of Loch Ness, Scotland, in 1985, is at the Brooklands Museum of Motor Sport and Aviation in Surrey.

For the duration of World War II, Bomber Command used the Wellington in a total of 47,409 operations in which they dropped 41,823 tonnes of bombs for a loss of 1332 planes. They were also used elsewhere. Coastal Command deployed 44 Wellingtons to Greece where they were used by the RAF during the Greek Civil War. The Hellenic Air Force also used them. Meanwhile, they were used by the RAF in battle in the Middle and Far East theatres, and the South African Air Force to repel the slower Italian planes.

In the 35 flights Bennett took in a Wellington (Marks I, II, III, and IV) at Church Broughton – day and night flights that ranged from one hour to five hours – he honed his crew-skippering skills by practising circuits and landings and simulated bombing raids as well as lifesaving emergency procedures such as parachute, dinghy and crash-landing drills. It soon became apparent that Bennett was a safe and trusted leader and Captain.

On 10 September he was promoted to Pilot Officer, and while his logbook assessment reads 'proficient', it was devoid of any inference of criticism.

Before flying the Avro Lancaster, Bennett and his crew had to fly together in the Halifax Mark V, in a process that included circuit flying and landings, and bomber and fighter affiliation. The Halifax was the first four-engine heavy bomber used by the RAF in the war, and like the Lancaster, required a crew of seven. It was far superior to the Wellington in all aspects, especially in all-important areas such as maximum speed (454 km/h), range (3000 km), ceiling (7315 m), and bomb-load (5897 kg). The crew was transferred to the Heavy Conversion Unit at Sandtoft, 7 kilometres south of Doncaster in southwest Lincolnshire, and remained there from October to mid-December.

Sandtoft had only just re-opened in May that year. And like many RAF bases in 'Bomber County' – as Lincolnshire became known – it is little used today other than as an airport for small commercial flights and as an industrial site. During the war though, Sandtoft was regarded as a vital base for airmen to fine-tune their operational training. The base was also nicknamed 'Prangtoft' because of the many aeroplane crashes that occurred there – as Bennett's crew discovered almost immediately. As they arrived, they were welcomed by the sight of five burning Lancasters on an airfield that, according to Henry Ford, was littered with pools of oil under the water. It was an ominous sight, for the crew's spell in Sandtoft was marked with a tragedy that Bennett would remember for the rest of his life – the death in a crash of his friend Alec Edmonds.

The tragedy was partly predicted by Bennett and his crew during a training flight one afternoon. As Ford recalls: 'It was going all right except that Keith had noticed the instrument that allows us to fly straight and level was working in reverse. In daylight that was all right, you could see your own wings and judge your own position. And if you were lucky, you could see the horizon. But even from the cloud layer you had an idea whether you were going straight and level or not.'

Bennett reported the irregularity, which could prove fatal for any crew flying at night, and the problem was fixed, as it was on other planes which had the same technical fault. But not all of the planes were repaired, Edmonds' kite being one of them. On 13 December 1944, Edmonds' bomber crashed into a farmhouse at Hatfield near Doncaster after taking off from Sandtoft at twilight. The accident killed Edmonds and two of his six-man crew. As Ford recalls, 'Alec wouldn't have had a clue if he was flying straight and level.' Bennett's sorrow for his mate's death was compounded by guilt for not pushing harder for a widespread technical overhaul when he first reported the problem. 'Keith always said afterwards that he wished he had taken a stronger stand,' Ford remembers. 'When Keith spoke to the engineer officer, this officer said, "Oh well, let's keep it quiet, shall we?" It was doubtlessly somebody's fault. And it was seen to afterwards, but too late for Alec Edmonds' crew.'

In hospital with chickenpox at the time, Ford was unable to join his crew to attend Edmonds' funeral, but the rest of them flew in their bomber to Montrose, Scotland, for the ceremony. They returned for their final week at Sandtoft heavy-hearted with their first first-hand experience of the high risks of crewing a bomber.

Edmonds would not be the last friend Bennett would lose during the war. Indeed, the likelihood of such a tragedy occurring meant that many pilots tried not to become too close to airmen outside of their crews. As for Bennett, the sorrow he felt for the mates he lost was deep and in 1947, after the war was over, he wrote to the parents of friends who'd died.

After 25 flights in the Halifax Mark V – fifteen of them as First Pilot – Bennett and his crew were ready for the final stage of their training: the Lancaster Finishing School.

Until now, many of the previous bombers had been known as 'Flying Coffins' – including the Lancaster's predecessor, the twin-engine Manchester that was also made by Avro – because of the numbers of them shot down. But the Avro Lancaster that had four Rolls Royce Merlin engines was rated the bomber of its time, challenged only by the Halifax. And despite imperfections that led to ten versions of the plane being made, it is still regarded as one of the greatest planes ever.

Following its first use in 1942, Lancasters went on to drop 608,612 tonnes of bombs from 156,000 operations until the war finished in 1945. Primarily a night bomber, its greatest feature was its massive bomb bay (10.05 m) that could hold a maximum load of 10,000 kg with the average being 6400 kg; and the maximum speed of 450 km/h, ceiling of 8160 metres and a range of travel of 4300 km that all helped to make it the ideal bomber for long incursions into German territory when it was needed to win the war.

The Lancaster also had an advanced communications system that comprised 1155 and 1154 transmitters that had direction finding, voice and Morse capabilities, and on-board defence of eight 0.303 Browning guns in three key areas: the nose, rear and mid-upper turrets. Over the course of the war, 7377 Lancasters were built at a cost of £45,000 (equivalent to £1.3–1.5m in 2005) each, of which 3249 were lost in action. Only 35 of them were flown in 100 or more operations, with the record being 139.

Of the seventeen that still exist – including 'G for George' that is on display at the Australian War Memorial Museum in Canberra, Australia – only two are airworthy. One is the PA474 that takes part in the annual Battle of Britain Memorial flight with 10 other aircraft: five Spitfires, two Hurricanes, one AC Douglas (DC3) AC-47 Dakota and two De Havilland Chipmunks. The other is FM213, which is kept at the Canada Warplane Heritage Museum and is known as the Mynarski

Memorial Lancaster in honour of Pilot Officer Andrew Mynarski and is also painted in the markings of his aircraft.

Bennett's experience of flying the Lancaster at the Lancaster Flying School numbered eight flights in Marks I and II, with four as first pilot.

On 29 December 1944, Bennett and his crew were deployed to the airbase at Binbrook. Like the rest of their colleagues, whether they were ready or not, no one knew. And nor would they until, for many of them, it was tragically too late.

YEAR		AIRCRAFT		Pilot, or 1st Pilot	2nd Pilot, Pupil or Passenger	DUTY (Including Results and Remarks)
Month	Date	Type	No.			
—	—	—	—	—	—	Totals Brought Forward
MAY	3	LANCASTER III	G₂	SELF	F/O EMERSON	30TH. OPERATION
					SGT ENTWISTLE	SUPPLY DROPPING NEAR
					F/S MURRAY	ROTTERDAM. 4 BLOCKS
					F/S FORD	OF 284 SACKS. 416 MLS
					F/S FREEZER	WEATHER STILL VERY
					F/S FIRKINS	SQUALLY

7. Lawrence S/L
O.C. 'C' FLIGHT

SUMMARY FOR MAY.   TYPES.
UNIT   460 SQUADRON   LANCASTER I
DATE   5.5.45   LANCASTER III
SIGNATURE

C.O. 460 SQUADRON.   W/C.

TOTAL HOURS FOR 460 SQUADRON.

Chapter 4

The Hunger Winter

'The farmers were hated. They made fortunes.
The little food that was left they would sell.'

Henk Benness

AFTER THE 'HUNGER WINTER' OF 1944, morale and health among the Dutch in western Holland was at its lowest ebb. Hundreds of the impoverished region's four million people were dying every day and thousands more were close to death as they fought the starvation and disease that had stricken the area. Forced to subsist on a daily diet of less than 500 calories – equal to a couple of potatoes and a portion of bread – many people were merely hanging onto their lives. They bore the tell-tale signs of famine victims – bloated bellies, swollen legs, sunken chests, and faces with large bulging eyes staring blankly as if in a trance. Medical supplies were rare; wood, coal and electricity virtually non-existent. And worse, it was also constantly cold, wet and dark.

In the months leading to that dreaded winter, the Allies believed that the war would be over by Christmas with the execution of Operation Market Garden – Field Marshal Montgomery's plan, which began on 17 September, to drop thousands of Allied paratroopers over southern Holland with the aim of pushing the Germans back.

The objective of Operation Market Garden was for three airborne divisions to take control of a select number of bridges behind enemy lines in the Netherlands and create a corridor for the British ground forces to follow from Belgium, through the Dutch towns of Eindhoven, Nijmegen and then to Arnhem where they would attempt to take the bridge that crossed the Rhine. From there the Allies would turn right and into the Ruhr, the industrial heart of Germany.

Though it did have its detractors – some wanted to free all of Holland first rather than drive east and push the German occupying forces backwards – the plan looked to be working when the Allies took the Waal Bridge at Nijmegen on 20 September. So confident were the Allies of pulling off their plan that the Dutch government still based in England urged a rail strike in Holland, believing that a strike would limit German mobility and stymie their chances of launching a counterattack.

The Dutch Resistance responded to their government's call and within 24 hours had managed to encourage all Dutch rail-workers to strike and go underground. The move was effective. For several days all was quiet due to the sudden stoppage of trains. But then the Germans responded by first re-assigning their own rail-workers from Germany to take up the strikers' work and then they hit back with force.

They ordered an immediate halt to all food transportation

for six weeks – a move that within days led to rationing and made food shortage inevitable. Those in the urban areas of western Holland felt the effects most severely; at least in the countryside people could rely on their own home-grown crops. Things didn't improve once the halt on food supplies was lifted. By this time, the canals had frozen over, preventing food transport barges from using their passage.

The German response to the rail strike was as physically brutal as it was bureaucratically cruel. Many Dutch people were shot, countless others taken away in what the Germans termed *razzias* – house-raids where any males over eighteen were sent away as forced labour to rebuild the ailing German defences on the Yssel River (or Yssel-line) that was regarded as an extension of the Siegfried Line. In some cases, entire families were thrown out of home. As is described by P.A. Donker in his book *Winter '44–'45 in Holland: A Winter Never to be Forgotten*:

In the south Holland islands, and in the coastal region, old men, women and children are turned out of their houses. Through rain and storm they march in endless columns along the roads. Vehicles, even perambulators, are taken away by the Germans. 'Why don't you go by train?' shouts a well-fed soldier scornfully at a little old woman toiling along. Fertile polders are being inundated. The supply of food stuffs is totally stopped. At Rotterdam and Amsterdam the thunder of heavy explosions resounds. Docks are being destroyed and sunk, harbour equipment and ship-yards – sources of prosperity – mercilessly blown up.

Donker recalls how Dr Arthur Seyss-Inquart, the Reichs-kommissar for the occupied Netherlands, gallingly declared in *Deutsche Zeitung in den Niederlanden* (the German newspaper published in the Netherlands): 'The transport of essential supplies to the west is a problem which must be solved by the Dutch themselves.'

As well as using force, the Germans devised a plan to recruit Dutch manpower to the Yssel River by deception and lies: they bribed the most starving among them to work for money. Overnight, the trap was set under the guise of Advice Bureau for Labour advertisements published in newspapers that advocated 'good care', 'high wages', and a 'satisfactorily organised postal service with relatives'. Another that was calling for workers living in – or those willing to move to – the Meppel and Groningen areas to the northeast, offered free accommodation and food rations. This included an extra allowance to send a bag of potatoes each week to their presumably starving families back home – a luxury indeed given, as Donker recalls: 'A potato coupon [bought] you one kilo of potatoes a week after four or five weeks have elapsed; oil, meat and vegetables [were] fond memories, just as sausage, jam or artificial honey.' Further stoking Dutch anger was that desperately needed foodstuffs were in plentiful supply, stored by the Germans for their exclusive use.

Despite its initial success, Operation Market Garden ultimately failed. In what came to be known as the last major victory by the Germans in their western campaign, the British 1st Division was defeated in the Battle of Arnhem. The failed operation effectively cut off western Holland. Four million Dutch had to deal with 15,000 occupying Germans who continued to plunder the region of all its remaining cultural, infrastructural, energy and human resources before their final retreat.

As September rolled into October, and October into November – the days getting shorter, darker and colder – the suffering among the Dutch in western Holland grew worse. Compounding the stark divide between the Dutch and Germans, divisions soon emerged among the Dutch too – between those who lived in the cities and those in country areas. Initially, food was scarcer in the cities due to congestion, the number of people, the squalor, the breakdown of resources and transport, and the fact that the Germans tended to plunder the cities first. By contrast, in the country people still had access to rural produce and livestock – that is, until the Germans stole those as well. Henk Benness, whose mother sold her wedding ring for food, recalls: 'People in the country, they usually have contacts and there was a lot of black markets. The farmers were hated. They made fortunes. The little food that was left, they would sell.'

In time, the Hunger Winter became a battle for survival for everyone. Officially, one needed a coupon for food and supplies, but soon enough these counted for nothing as supplies dwindled. The Dutch were forced to become as resourceful as possible, making use of whatever they could find for food and energy supplies; nothing was wasted. They supplemented their meagre rations with recipes rich in sugar beet, such as the sugar beet pancakes that became the household 'specialty' of the Van Splunders in Ridderkerk; or potato peels and tulip bulbs that had to be boiled, peeled and the poisonous heart extracted before being eaten. Even grass was plucked from the garden and then boiled in hot water to make a broth. The shortage of meat meant that many families had no option but to sacrifice their beloved family pets, not to mention their livestock if it hadn't already been stolen by the Germans.

No distance was too great for them as they set off in the cold and wet on food-seeking missions. Travelling by foot or by bicycle on wet and muddied country tracks hardened by dangerous black ice, these journeys became known as the 'hunger marches', pitiable experiences which broke the mind as much as the body.

Freek Jansen gives a vivid first-hand account of the struggle, suffering and hazards in *Winter '44–'45 in Holland – a Winter Never to be Forgotten*. A former employee in the Netherlands Shipbuilding Yard, Jansen describes one such journey with about a thousand Dutchmen from Amsterdam to the north of Holland – a 100 km round trip – on foot and on bikes with bare rims in rain. Many did not make it home, dying of starvation, disease or exhaustion along the way. Upon learning they were from Amsterdam, many country folk closed their doors to them. By this point, the city-dwelling Dutch were desperate to find food. Forced from their homes in search of food, they expected sympathy and more plentiful supplies of food in the country, as produce was being grown and livestock raised at the farms. Instead they were often confronted by a rural population that was not only wary of the Germans who had occupied their villages and plundered their natural resources, but also suspicious of a city populace they feared would do the same. Their desperation was understandable considering the starvation; but it often led to thuggery and theft – even to the slaughtering of the livestock of those few country folk who were hospitable to them. In the words of Jansen:

This is hell: benumbed feet in sopping shoes, lashing rain, ice, wind and a burden heavy as lead and gloomy darkness around. A cycle-wheel that breaks down, weariness that leads to a swoon and in all this chilling rain a burning thirst, thirst and a knowing sensation of hunger . . . After an hour, after half an hour, the potato-haulers must be indoors. But nobody knows how far it is yet. The rain comes down in torrents on a road that seems already half-submerged. 'Hello is anybody there? Hello, just answer!'

Right in front of us raucous curses are heard and behind us an anxious voice whispers a doleful prayer: 'God, don't let that rim break now! I am thirsty, hungry. I can go no further . . . How am I to get home?' Is this a nightmare or is it raw reality? We are all too fully aware that it is reality and we know also that we want to sleep for three days and for three nights at a stretch. Just to wake up for a moment to eat our fill with the spuds we brought along and then to sleep on, to snooze in the safe protection of a warm pit . . . But we shan't be home for the present!

What does it matter if we stand in the midst of a puddle with bent backs? Does a drowning man care whether water is grey or green? He lets himself down and hears the angels singing in the back of his head. This is what the end must be like.

However, as Henk Benness reveals, even shorter trips for food offered plenty of risks, as he found during one outing with his mother. It was a bitterly cold afternoon when they set off from their home in Gouda on their bikes, on a mission to buy milk from a farm 4 kilometres away. As they always did before any ride in such cold conditions, they shoved a thick layer of paper under their clothes to keep warm and donned big mittens, hats and their thickest coats. Upon arriving at the farm, they saw about thirty people already standing and shaking in the cold next to a bridge that adjoined the road to the farm. Underneath the bridge was a large ditch. It soon became clear that the ditch had a purpose. It was there to fend off impatient and quickly freezing customers until the farmer was ready to roll out his urn and sell his milk – frequently having to mix it with water to meet demand. Often, the wait would be for over an hour, further exacerbating the frustration of customers. As Benness remembers: 'My mother was at the front of the line and some-body pushed her. With her heavy clothing she fell into the ditch. We had to pull her out before she froze. But the farmer took pity, took her inside the house and put her in front of a fire. He then gave her a litre of milk and also free washing.'

The shortage of wood and coal, and the need for heating and

cooking facilities, drove the Dutch to further acts of desperation. The most obvious source of fuel was wood, which led many people to break up and store pieces of unnecessary furniture or doors. But it wasn't long before wood too became scarce. Many were then prepared to risk the danger of being shot by the Germans by breaking the 8 pm curfew; some even braved the freezing winter nights and rowed out to one of the islets that littered the region to cut down trees for wood. Many were also willing to endanger their lives by chasing the German-run trains in the hope that goods and coal would fall off the back and onto the tracks. This was especially risky because the RAF Spitfires would, without warning, swoop down and fire upon the trains, track-lines, or anything else under German control.

Benness recalls facing the danger: 'Anything that moved from that railway line was shot at,' he says, adding that he will never forget the fear of being caught in Allied cross-fire. This often happened during the food trips he took with his mother. 'This bloody Spitfire spears down the main road. There were German cars and Germans flew out. Along the road they had these viaducts you could dive into. You went in head first, but were sheltered and away you went again. But it was not what you'd call a very safe sort of journey. They were really into the business.'

Meanwhile, the humble potato became a pricey item on the black market when supply lines to Drenthe, northeast of Amsterdam – where potatoes lay rotting in the ground uncollected – were either cut, became impossible to travel on due to lack of petrol and vehicles, or were simply frozen over. And when the Germans continued to claim that the shortage in western Holland was a Dutch problem, not theirs, 2170 men one night risked crossing the Zuyder-zee by boat to collect potatoes and extra coal in Drenthe, despite German threats to take as forced labour anyone who attempted the trip.

With 700 tonnes of potatoes plucked from 200 hectares of land, the food was ready to be transported to needy areas. But the Dutch were informed in *De Telegraaf* newspaper – then run by the Germans – that they would have to ship the produce themselves. As the newspaper reported: 'We have been authorised by the German authorities to state that between 100,000 and 200,000 tonnes of Dutch inland shipping space is available for the transport of food supplies to the large cities of north Holland, south Holland and Utrecht. They will render all possible facilities, but only adhere to the condition that all this has to be carried out by the Dutch themselves.'

On the day the above notice was published, two ships laden with potatoes were stopped by German vessels near Amsterdam. The Germans seized all the cargo, threw off the crews and took control of the ships that would then be used to transport back to Germany whatever remaining supplies the Germans could plunder from the Netherlands.

The potato swindle was not the only instance of the Germans halting an approved humanitarian effort. On 26 January 1945, two Swedish Red Cross vessels bound for the port of Marsdiep, north of Amsterdam, carrying 3600 tonnes of food for children and hospital patients were confronted by a German naval vessel. The Swedish ships were forced to alter course back to Delfzijl, northeast of Groningen. From there, transport of the supplies by water was impossible due to hardened winter ice. Again, the starving in western Holland had to wait – until the ice melted, or 'an opportunity of railway transport through Dutch initiative arises,' reported *De Telegraaf*.

The Dutch also soon learned that the offer from the German-run Advice Bureau for Labour of ample food and good accommodation and wages was nothing but lies. Desperate with hunger, many Dutch took up the opportunity, despite efforts by the Dutch Resistance to discourage their recruitment with orange posters depicting a bent-over worker digging under the eye of a knife-wielding German with the words: 'Are you the enemy's slave? Then report yourselves for labour! If not, then don't!' But as Donker suggests, the call to resist the Germans for patriotic reasons was not always the most practical one. 'If not, then starve,' is the catch-cry he suggests should have appeared on those posters.

According to Donker, about 300 people a week lined up at the Advice Bureau for Labour's Amsterdam office, citing as an example an 'Uncle Dorus', a seaman sent back to Amsterdam after breaking his leg, who earned his keep doing odd jobs around the shipyards or working for the Salvation Army until the Hunger Winter deprived him of all work and left him on the breadline, starving. Donker describes Dorus signing up with two others to work for the Germans at Port Natal. He is convinced his fortune has changed when he is immediately given a serving of bread and butter with sausage, and a mug of hot coffee before being shown to a warm bed of straw to sleep it off. The following day he is told he will earn five guilders a day –

with two-and-a-half extra on Sunday. Soon enough, he is hard at work digging ditches. But he hates the job, the soreness, hates it all, and opts to leave with three others one night after claiming three days' ration of bread, butter and sausage.

But even 'volunteers' cannot leave, as Uncle Dorus discovers. He is shot. And as Donker writes: 'The following day, a hundred diggers from Port Natal under an armed guard are compelled to march past the spot where "Teutonic" justice has been done: a warning example to other volunteers who might want to run away from their good employment.'

The crisis did provide some opportunities for black humour, as Henk Benness admits – albeit in retrospect. It was Christmas 1944, a typically cold night, with black ice thick on the roads. There was no coal in the Benness house to warm the room or even stoke a fire in the small pot-belly stove that was used for cooking and heating. Benness' uncle had an idea. 'We'll beat those bloody bastards,' he told his nephew. So the pair got on their bikes and rode the short distance to a hospital where the Germans were known to have stored coal near a wall cordoned off with barbed wire and guarded by a sentry in a watch-house. 'A cousin of mine lived opposite in a small house with a small front garden and he had a hedge,' recalls Benness. 'The first thing we did when we arrived was put our bikes behind the hedge and observe what the Germans were doing. Since it was Christmas, they were drinking and getting merry and singing. We waited until they were *really* singing.'

In time, the German chorus attracted other Dutch neighbours who, like Benness, had all heard of the prized booty lying in a pile on the other side of the hedge. Together, they waited . . . and waited, as the merry German sentries sang and drank themselves silly.

Then when the Germans had finally fallen asleep, Benness and the other younger Dutch boys – all carrying jute bags – were lifted up and over the hedge to raid the stock.

'But as soon as you step on coke it makes a terrible noise,' says Benness. 'So it was as if there was a bloody volcano. All this coke went into the bags, back to the fence and over the fence. In no time we had about three of those bags.'

But suddenly they were in very real danger as the noise woke one of the sentries. 'The next minute the door of the watch-house flew open and this German came out and he was swaying,' explains Benness. 'He had a machine gun and he shot it in the air. He didn't shoot at us fortunately. I've never been as quick over a fence in my life, and all these little boys ran over. So for about a week we had coke.'

So the black humour?

Many years later, while on holidays with his wife and kids and staying at a chateau in the Black Forest, Benness met a German man who recognised his accent and knew his home-town of Gouda very well. 'He said, "Do you know such-and-such square and the hospital?" I replied that I did. He said, "I was one of those soldiers in that watch-house." These days he was a big wheel in some winery and he promised to send us a crate of wine and some goblets, which he did. When we came back home a few months later, there they were.'

YEAR		AIRCRAFT		Pilot, or	2nd Pilot, Pupil	DUTY
Month	Date	Type	No.	1st Pilot	or Passenger	(Including Results and Remarks)
—		—	—	—	—	Totals Brought Forward
May	3	LANCASTER III	G²	SELF	F/O EMERSON	30TH. OPERATION
					SGT ENTWISTLE	SUPPLY DROPPING NEAR
					F/S MURRAY	ROTTERDAM. 4 BLOCKS
					F/S FORD	OF 284 SACKS. 416 MLS
					F/S FREEZER	WEATHER STILL. VERY
					F/S FIRKINS	SQUALLY

F. Lawrence S/L
O.C. 'C' FLIGHT

W/C
C.O. 460 SQUADRON.

SUMMARY FOR. MAY.
UNIT   460 SQUADRON
DATE   5.5.45
SIGNATURE   KW Benn ??

TYPES.
LANCASTER I
LANCASTER III

TOTAL HOURS FOR 460 SQUADRON.

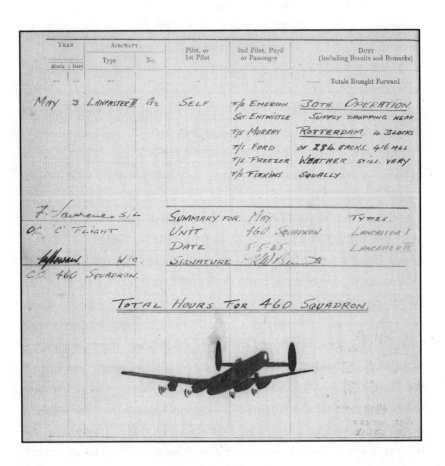

Chapter 5

Binbrook: Home Away From Home

Quite often we would say: 'Well, bugger this, I'm not going to shower in the cold' and we wouldn't shower for a couple of days.

Henry Ford

IT'S OVER SIXTY YEARS SINCE THE END OF THE WAR, and green grass now pushes through the old abandoned concrete runways of the Binbrook airbase in Lincolnshire. Looking back at the massive green hangars that are still there but empty of planes, it is easy to imagine row upon row of Lancaster bombers, their four powerful Rolls-Royce Merlin-engined propellers spinning in readiness for take-off. Inside sit the seven crewmen – most an average age of twenty years – about to embark on yet another risky mission over the skies of Europe.

Binbrook was one of the most important of the hundreds of RAF airbases that littered Lincolnshire. Higher than most bases, it sits on top of a plateau on the chalk foundations of the Lincolnshire 'wolds' of northeast England, the runway constantly exposed to the stiff and cold winds that blow off the North Sea and from as far away as Siberia. Surrounding the base are waves of hills and farmlands that make up a patchwork of lush green crops and yellow buttercups which provide food for the grazing cattle. Below the former airbase, one kilometre to the northwest, is the village of Binbrook from where the steeple of the parish church, St Mary and St Gabriel, still protrudes as prominently today as it did during the war when it served as a beacon for returning bomber crews.

Binbrook was home to many RAF squadrons during the war – including 460 Squadron – and the village was regularly populated by up to 2500 people. The first plane – a Fairey Battle light bomber piloted by Flying Officer Doug Gosman – landed there in June 1940, leading the impending arrival of 12 and 142 Squadrons. The base operated until June 1988 when it was forced to close due to defence cuts. Its closure was not taken lightly. After operating for nearly half a century, the presence and influence of the RAF have given the village and its environs an extremely rich culture and history.

Today, each squadron that has ever been based at Binbrook is honoured inside St Mary and St Gabriel Catholic Church, its name and motto etched on a stained-glass window erected the year after the airbase folded. Named the Royal Air Force Memorial Window, it holds premier place in the ancient walls of the southern side of the church, near the front of the first pew. Three metres tall by one metre wide, it is adorned with images and etchings that marry both the military and religious significance of the RAF's union with the village.

An explanation of the window's etchings shows:

- The quatrefoil (at top): contains flames that symbolise the fire of the Holy Spirit.
- The left-hand lancet (from top): the dove, depicting the Holy Spirit, purity and peace; the famed Fairey Battle light bomber that was the first plane to land in Binbrook; the Shield of Angel Gabriel, one of the patrons of the church; the lily, the symbol of the annunciation of Our Lady, connecting with the chapel and the deification of the church; the station crest of RAF Binbrook and then the dedication that reads: *To the glory of God in commemoration of the life and work of RAF Binbrook 1940–1988 and in gratitude for the help and support in the village.*
- The right-hand lancet (from top): the Lancaster; the Lightning; the church of St Mary and St Gabriel, sited within the crossing of the two runways signifying the link between the base and village; the poppy, in remembrance of those who died in the service of the RAF at Binbrook; the shield of St Michael, symbolising the light and victory of good over evil; and also the station church of Binbrook.
- The rainbow swirl at centre forms a union between two lights and serves as a formal speed device, especially with regard to the Lightning emerging from the speed window.
- At the end of the runway, patterns symbolise Christ, the

guiding light and being five in number remind us also of the five wounds of Christ.

- In the background is a composition of the field pattern around the airfield as seen from the air which includes the pattern of hangar roofs as seen from above.
- In the lower third of the lancets are recorded the squadrons that served at RAF Binbrook with dates of duty – a symbol of all the work carried out on the base by the RAF and civilians to fulfil their function of defending the United Kingdom in peace and war.

No squadron is honoured more than 460 Squadron. As well as their names being etched on the window, nearby is an honour roll that lists those who lost their lives in the war. It sits below another plaque on the wall that pays tribute to 460 Squadron. Next to the honour roll is a poem written by Geoff Magee which honours those in the Squadron killed in action. Titled 'To Absent Friends of 460 Squadron', it reads:

Age shall not weary them, nor the years condemn
So truly says the Ode.
And as we age, we think of them
For whom life's course has flowed.

Some died still boys in cruel war,
For some the tears have not yet dried,
But all have given us a store
Of memories, to recall with pride

Of Ops we shared, and the life we knew,
And the squadron where we tried
To strike and return each time we flew,
But sadly, where many died

Sometimes I hope that when I die
There will come a ghostly Lanc,
Winging through the night time sky
To land on a soft cloud bank

And out will step some Angels,
And those Angels all will be
Those squadron mates of every rank,
Come to escort me

And the pains of age will leave me,
As through the skies we soar,
With the sounds of Angels singing,
And the Merlin's ghostly roar

If this poem doesn't reflect strongly enough the deep regard in which 460 Squadron is held in Binbrook, then the one-metre-tall stone memorial at the village entrance surely does. Sitting on a grassy street corner on the road to the town of Market Rasen, flowers are regularly placed at its base.

After the RAF moved out of Binbrook, the land was sold to Charles Nickerson, who in turn sold off much as a housing estate now called Brookenby. The hangars went to small industry in need of storage space. Today, the front sign at the former base's gates reads: *Binbrook Trade Estate*, and in place of squadron insignia are the logos of some of the industrial businesses that operate there, such as the Dyno Centre (a motorcycle-testing facility), Winchester Marine, and Classic Furniture.

Apart from the overgrown runways, all that remains of the site's history as one of the most strategic airbases of Bomber Command are the faded green hangars whose giant sliding doors are closed, Nissen huts that were used as accommodation by flight and ground crews and the WAAF (Women's Auxiliary Air Force), several small traffic control towers whose broken windows indicate their neglect, and one wash-grey Lightning jet from the 1980s that sits next to trucks and tractors under a tarpaulin held down by giant tractor tyres to prevent the North Sea winds from blowing it away. These days, Binbrook base is more of a ghost town rather than a place of homage to those airmen and women who served in the forces. With the close of the base, Binbrook and many villages like it – such as Market Rasen and Grimsby – have suffered downturns in their economies. Undoubtedly, these places once owed much to the squadrons that made the villages their home.

There is one pub in Binbrook – the Harrow and Plough – rather than the two it had until the Marquis of Granby, a popular public house for the RAF, was turned into a listed and restored house in 1999. During the war, the Marquis of Granby was the closer of the two pubs to the RAF airbase 2 kilometres away. The pub was then run by Rene Trevor, the wife of an RAF airman who had been sent to serve in the Middle East.

For many Binbrook-based airmen, Rene became a mother as much as a publican. Coming from a pub family – her father owned the Crown Inn in her hometown of Tealby for 43 years – Rene loved running the establishment. Besides pulling beers and serving meals for tired crew, she spent many an evening sewing on buttons and decorations and mending their jackets. She has strong memories of those first days in 1940 when the RAF came to town. As she recalled in *The Evening Standard*'s special 'Farewell to Binbrook' liftout: 'They had been in France only a few days before and all they had was what they arrived in . . . That night some of them came down to the Granby and I remember them saying, "A real English pub with a piano – can you play it?"' Rene did play, and she sang as well. That night the tunes and chorus-lines of such wartime greats as 'Cowboy Joe', 'I like Merlin Music' and 'Goodnight Sweetheart' resonated throughout the pub as clients drank merrily, signalling the beginning of the relationship between the pub and Bomber Command.

During her time running the Marquis of Granby, Rene Trevor had no choice but to become accustomed to the raw reality of war. Airmen often took solace in establishments such as hers upon hearing of the death of a mate. 'The lads used to get very low at times,' she said. 'But they brightened up after a few drinks and a sing-song around the piano.'

As they did when crews finished their tour of operations, which amounted to 30 sorties. Upon reaching that score, each crew member would be held aloft to sign his name on the pub ceiling. 'I kept that ceiling like it was until we left the Granby in 1949, but the next people in just covered the names up,' said Rene.

Rene remembers that April day when the Australians swooped into Binbrook in their Lancasters. 'My daughter Anne was about three at the time and we had just begun telling her about the war and about the Germans. One day she came running through the front bar screaming: "Mummy, Mummy, the Germans are here." She had just heard an Australian accent for the first time.'

Rene's daughter was popular among the Australians, who often asked her to sing to them. They also showed her their mischievous side, as Rene recalled of one incident that involved their pet donkey who was kept behind the pub. 'One night some of the lads got a bit tight [drunk] and they took the donkey with them back up to the sergeants' mess. They brought it back the next day. Quite apologetic, they were.'

First to arrive among the Australians was an advance party from 460 Squadron then led by the highly decorated and extroverted Group Captain Hughie Edwards, who would become the third highest decorated airforce officer in the war – after Wing Commanders Leonard Cheshire VC, DSO, DFC and Guy Gibson VC, DSO, DFC – and would thus become an Air Commodore himself and retire with a VC, DSO, DFC after his name.

By the time of Edwards' arrival in Binbrook, he already held Britain's highest military award for courage – the Victoria Cross – earned on 22 July 1941 just eighteen days after being awarded a Distinguished Flying Cross while holding rank as Wing Commander of 105 Squadron flying Blenheim bombers from East Anglia. He was awarded a VC for his role in a day-light raid on the port of Bremen which he executed with daring panache. In January 1943, shortly before arriving at Binbrook, Edwards earned a Distinguished Service Order while leading a formation of Mosquito fighter planes in a daylight raid on the Philips radio factory in Eindhoven, a feat that saw him promoted to Group Captain a month later and assigned his two-year post as Commanding Officer of the first Australian Lancaster squadron – 460 Squadron.

The squadron was part of Bomber Command, which was then divided into seven groups – No. 6 Group being the Royal Canadian Air Force; 5 Group from Scampton in central Lincolnshire to Woodall Spa in the south; 4 Group, in north and east Yorkshire; 3 Group, in Suffolk, Cambridgeshire and Bedfordshire; 2 Group (later 100 Group), in North Norfolk; and 1 Group, to which 460 Squadron belonged, south of the Humber in north Lincolnshire. The last group was 8 Group – the elite Pathfinder force that was located at its headquarters in Huntingdon, Cambridgeshire.

The 460 Squadron was one of eight Australian squadrons that served Bomber Command in World War II, although some were transferred to other posts, such as 455 Squadron that was re-assigned to Coastal Command after its 1941–42 spell in Bomber Command; 458 Squadron that was transferred to the Middle East after 1941; and 464 Squadron that joined Second Tactical Air Force following its 1942–43 spell.

The mission of Edwards' advance party was to prepare the base for the transfer of their Lancaster Mark Is from RAF

Breighton, near York, on 4 May. When the big day arrived, 250 aircrew came to Binbrook by Lancasters, while another 150 made the trip by overland vehicles. Another 868 personnel were flown in by Horsa gliders that also transported 90 tonnes of equipment. It took four days for 460 Squadron to set itself up. By 23 May, they were on their first operation to Dortmund.

On that day, the newly arrived Australians were visited by King George VI and Queen Elizabeth during their Royal tour of the Lincolnshire airbases. The Royals spent an hour at the base which by then housed 2370 RAF personnel that included 330 WAAFs. The King and Queen met twelve crews from 460 Squadron and twelve from 100 Squadron which had been based at Binbrook's satellite bases of Wickenby and Grimbsy.

Later that night, the mood of celebration following the high-profile meeting was stymied when one of those who met the Royals – Pilot Officer Harrison – was killed in a raid on Essen.

Throughout the rest of 1943 and into 1944, many, many more Binbrook airmen would be killed. Also during this time, 460 Squadron's reputation – and those of the Australians who were a part of it – only grew. Edwards, who had Air Commodore Arthur Wray as Binbrook's base commander, typically led from the front. Senior officers like him were discouraged from flying missions, but he regularly participated, even doing so under a false name to avoid being detected. His tactic was a morale-booster, showing the squadron's aircrews that he would not ask of his crew what he was not willing to do himself.

In September 1943, Binbrook was visited by the commander-in-chief of Bomber Command, Air Marshal Arthur Harris, the

man behind the mass bombing of Germany and later to be titled
Air Chief Marshal Sir Arthur Harris. To this day, he is a controversial figure – loved by many, but also hated for the death and
destruction caused by his 'carpet bombing' policy. Harris' faith
in such tactics was influenced by what he believed was the total
ineffectiveness of precision bombing during the early years of
the war and saw him appointed as head of Bomber Command

During his visit, Harris – aka 'Bomber' Harris – met crews
from Binbrook, Wickenby and Grimsby, and witnessed a
demonstration of 'window dropping', window being the thin
aluminium strips that were released from the Lancasters during
bombing raids to confuse the German radar systems.

Throughout the next three months – from late November,
into December and January 1944 – between 200 and 1000 planes
took off each night to enact bombing raids over Berlin. Reports
of heroics by various crews increased, but sadly, so too did the
death-rates and plane losses. Many more went unreported.

As 460 Squadron's reputation blossomed, the mythology
surrounding some of its bombers grew. Many of them were shot
down, crashed into each other, were struck by bombs accidentally dropped by their own, or went missing in action after
only their first few operations. Mysteriously, other Lancasters
survived almost unscathed, the most notorious being 'G for
George' – officially registered as Mk 1 AR-G.

Built in 1942, she flew her first mission over Mannheim on
6 December of that year. But soon after being transferred from
Breighton to Binbrook, 'G for George' became known as a truly
'Lucky Lanc', even if she was holed by flak ten times in her first

30 operations. By the time she had flown her last operation on 20 April 1944 in a raid over Cologne, she had amassed 90 operations for 668 hours of flying time shared by 27 crews. Her reputation had spread back to Australia and it was decided she should be flown there. An all-RAAF crew of Bomber Command veterans was assigned to fly 'G for George' back to Australia where the plan was for her to be used in a nationwide publicity trip to boost the sale of war bonds that helped raise funds for the war effort. On 20 May that year, 'G for George' was officially handed over to the Australian prime minister, John Curtin, and nine days later was flown to Prestwick for an overhaul before the 20,000 km flight to Australia via Montreal, San Francisco, Hawaii, Fiji and New Caledonia. Incredibly, after the war she was left abandoned and in the open air at RAAF Base Fairbairn near Canberra until 1955 when, thankfully, she was moved to the Australian War Memorial in Canberra. In 2003, 'G for George' was re-built piece by piece to her wartime configuration and today hangs in the ANZAC Hall at the war memorial as a centrepiece of a sound and light show that superbly depicts a wartime bombing raid, also using a Luftwaffe BF-109 fighter and German '88' flak gun and background film imagery from a bombing raid. The dramatic storyline is based on the true events of a sortie captained by Flying Officer 'Cherry' Carter to Berlin on 'Black Thursday' 1943, when 50 of the 500 bombers sent out by Bomber Command were lost.

When Keith Bennett and his crew arrived at Binbrook from

William George Bennett: *The NCO Pilot, RFC*, painted by Sir William Orpen. During World War I Bennett snr accrued 300 hours of flying time in the skies over France.

Ready and willing: Keith Bennett signed with the Air Training Corps in September 1942.

On 2 January 1943 Keith Bennett enlisted as RAAF Airman 432472.

Before flying the Lancaster, Bennett and his crew took the Halifax to the skies. Left to right: Cyril Entwistle, Peter Firkins, Keith Bennett, Les Emmerson, Harold 'Henry' Ford, Alby Murray and Alex Freezer.

At last the Avro Lancaster was theirs to fly. Left to right: Alex Freezer, Harold 'Henry' Ford, Les Emmerson, Alby Murray, Cyril Entwistle, Keith Bennett, Peter Firkins.

Keith Bennett: the death of his friend Alec Edmonds, whose bomber crashed into a house, affected him greatly.

Alec Edmonds with a friend.

Off on another operation: rear gunner Peter Firkins and mid-upper gunner Alex Freezer.

Keith Bennett (right) and colleagues enjoy the quiet time between 'ops'.

December 1944 at the Heavy Conversion Unit (HCU) at
Sandtoft, near Doncaster: Peter Firkins (left), Les Emmerson
(centre) and Keith Bennett (right) with two Bat-girls, Penny
(left) and Molly (right). The toy kangaroo in Penny's hands is
Bennett's mascot, 'Joe'.

'Joe', Keith Bennett's mascot that
went with him on all operations
for good luck. Afterwards, Bennett
had the name of each target sewn
onto 'Joe'.

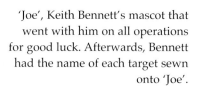

The 1000 bomber raids turned the tide of the war in favour of the Allies.

Bombing up: once the order was given, no matter the conditions, it was carried out. Here a 4000 lb 'Cookie' is delivered.

2 March 1945: 700 Lancasters and Halifaxes took part in the bombing of Cologne. Keith Bennett's G2 was one of them. This is the aerial shot taken from his bomber after dropping their bombs.

All but Cologne Cathedral was obliterated on 2 March 1945 . . .

. . . not that the interior of the cathedral was spared.

Return to base: Keith Bennett (left) pilots the G2 back to Binbrook after the bombing raid on Essen on 10 March 1945. On his right is flight engineer Cyril Entwistle.

The flight instrument panel of a Lancaster bomber.

The German pocket battleship Admiral Scheer lying with upturned keel in a dock basin at Kiel. She was sunk a month ago by R.A.F. Bomber Command.

Allied Fleet Of 48 Ships Off Oslo

AN Allied naval force of 48 ships has been sighted at the entrance to Oslo Fiord, the Swedish radio said last night, quoting telephone reports from Oslo, the Norwegian capital. "There are no reports that troops have been landed but it is expected that this will take place at any moment," the radio added.

The German heavy cruiser Prinz Eugen and the light cruiser Nuremberg have surrendered to Field-Marshal Montgomery's forces, with 160,000 tons of merchant shipping, it was officially announced last night.

Both the Prinz Eugen and the Nuremberg were in Copenhagen harbour recently.

Stalin announced in an Order of the Day last night that Breslau, the fortress town in Eastern Germany, had been captured.

The long awaited sinking of the *Admiral Scheer* on 9 April 1945 was confirmed to all in this newspaper article.

The *Admiral Scheer,* from above, after being bombed in the raid over Kiel in which Keith Bennett's crew took part.

How *The Daily Sketch* splashed the news of the bombing of Berchtesgaden on 25 April 1945.

En route to Berchtesgaden: 'It was a lovely day, hardly a cloud around and we were rumbling across sleepy little villages . . .' – Cyril Entwistle

On approach: 'I thought, "We are putting the fear of God into all these people. They know bloody well we are all laden with bombs."' – Cyril Entwistle

The aftermath: The first pictures of Berchtesgaden's bombing made front-page news in the *Sunday Express*.

Hitler's Berghof is bombed.

The Van Splunders at home in Ridderkerk (left to right): Jannie's father, Henri Arie; her twin sisters, Rookje and Wilhelmina; Jannie; and her mother, Wilhelmina.

Best friends: Bouvine Van Vliet (left) and Jannie Van Splunder (right). Both would write letters to Keith Bennett and Alby Murray, thanking them for Operation Manna.

Church Broughton on 1 January 1945, they were aware of 460 Squadron's reputation – although not yet fully educated about its real status. 'We learnt pretty quickly about the tradition,' said Bennett's wireless operator 'Henry' Ford, adding that during their training they'd heard about such decorated airmen from 460 Squadron as Wing Commanders Leonard Cheshire and Guy Gibson, and Group Captain Hughie Edwards. 'These fellows were great heroes.'

According to Ford, 460 Squadron was known as the 'Women's Weekly' Squadron because of its popularity as a subject in the Australian magazine that is still published as a monthly today. When the squadron was dismissed after its last parade at the end of the war, *The Australian Women's Weekly* was there to report the occasion. As Ford pointed out, 460 Squadron 'flew more operations than any other squadron, dropped more bombs – this is including English squadrons – lost more planes and had more decorations than any other squadron'. More poignantly perhaps, 460 Squadron also lost more lives than any other squadron. Bennett's crew played its own role in the history of 460 Squadron for the Lancaster they flew was G2, the replacement for 'G for George'. Though they played around with the idea of naming her – Bennett proposed Gundagai George, but it was rejected by his crew as 'too common' – in the end they never followed the tradition of naming their 'kite'.

Upon their arrival at Binbrook, Bennett's crew was split up to live in various quarters. Because they were commissioned officers, Bennett and navigator Les Emmerson were allocated quarters in a separate brick-built block which had far better conditions and benefits. The rest of them slept in another block: Alby Murray, Cyril Entwistle and Henry Ford were allocated one room to share, while Peter Firkins and Alex Freezer took another room.

At first glance, the living quarters appeared comfortable and well appointed for the wintry months that greeted them – unlike the basic Nissen huts that were more like garage sheds and offered for heating only a pot-bellied furnace that doubled as a clothes-dryer and cooker. 'They looked pretty good because downstairs you could light a fire. There was a hot-water service and you could use the bathroom upstairs to shave in. But little did we know that there was no fuel to burn in the fire, so we had no hot-water service. The water was also frozen, so some of the wiser guys would walk up a couple of hundred yards to the mess all rugged up, and use hot water from there, and the soap and showers there,' recalls Ford. Like his crewmates in the same block, he would often wear his 'warm' pyjamas under his RAF uniform to keep warm.

Showering was so bone-chilling that the crew members would sometimes skip washing. 'Quite often we would say: "Well, bugger this, I'm not going to shower in the cold" and we wouldn't shower for a couple of days.' Going to the toilet was not an easy process either. 'The toilets would ice over, and it was very uncomfortable and not very sanitary. You had to do your business on a sheet of ice. Then the toilet paper would run out, so you'd have some map of Europe or something – some navigation paper,' says Ford.

It was a different story for Bennett and Emmerson, though.

As commissioned officers they enjoyed hot water and heating in their quarters. Officers also had at their disposal the services of the WAAF – known as Bat-girls – who, among other tasks, would prepare their water for shaving, make their beds with clean sheets, and cook food that was in more plentiful supply and of far better quality. When drinking in the officers' mess, officers were also allowed to keep a tab running, although they were encouraged to pay up before an operation.

Despite their varying ranks, the crew on G2 – like most crews on the Australian squadron – greeted each other on first-name basis. Such familiarity, Entwistle notes, was more an Australian custom than an English RAF one where things were much more formal. 'The discipline was easier than in the RAF. In the Air Force you all "sir-red" and stuck into attention. But when flying, if I had anything to report, like battle damage or anything, I would report it by going on the intercom and saying: "engineer to pilot and crew" to pick their ears up.'

Such familiarisation among crew members did not mean they would always socialise together. Bennett, being a quieter and more reserved person whose calm demeanour was a much-valued trait in the air, would often spend his free time in London watching shows or musicals, or visiting family friends or relatives like his Auntie Nellie and Uncle Bill. Between operations he would regularly write letters home and update his diary.

Not that he would never indulge in a drink. To be sure, Bennett liked a tipple. And with the threat of death so prevalent for any airman, most social outings – especially with groups from a squadron – were unsurprisingly seized upon as vital opportunities to enjoy life as much as possible. And the amusing antics of what went on in the many pubs across Lincolnshire are as much a part of World War II folklore as are the frightening battles that raged high in the skies above Europe. One night their ears may have been numb from the sound of flak and battle, the next they would be ringing from laughter, debate and tomfoolery.

The Australians were well reputed for setting high social standards, as one former English airman, Fred Armstrong, fondly recalled in *The Evening Standard*'s 1988 'Farewell to Binbrook' liftout: 'They were very good chaps to get on with and whenever they had a stand-down they really let their hair down. Their philosophy was "make merry tonight for tomorrow we die", and sadly, that was often the case. Some of the things they got up to was no one's business.'

Bennett's crew would frequently drink at one of the messes at Binbrook where gatherings would often be highlighted by mass singalongs like those that were heard inside the Village Inn – built in 1943 next to the officers' mess and named as such because it resembled an English tavern. It was paid for by the mess, who also maintained it whenever the squadron was not busy. One of the most popular singalongs was that led by Squadron Leader 'Foggo' Lawrence, whose favourite rendition was 'The Muffin Man'. While singing and balancing a jug of beer on his bald head at the same time, Lawrence – no matter what gender of audience was before him – would brazenly strip down to his polka-dot boxer shorts that had a black Swastika on the backside. There were many more such drunken stunts – for example, adorning the interior of the Village Inn or the mess with footprints up the wall, right across the ceiling and down the other side. As Ford recalls, 'They dipped somebody's feet in beer or some sort of concoction, then walked them up and brought them down again.' On many occasions the G2 crew – like many Binbrook crews – would ride their bikes into the village for a drinking session at the Harrow and Plough or the Marquis of Granby, or they would take the short bus-trip to the seaside town of Grimsby to drink at their favourite pub, the Black Swan, better known as the 'Mucky Duck'.

'It was a matter of going wherever you could to get a drink because beer was in bloody short supply,' says Entwistle. 'Once [at the Black Swan], Alby and I wouldn't let the waitress take the bottles back. And at the end of the night there were 63 bottles there.'

Later, despite his blurred vision as they waited at the bus-stop for a ride back to Binbrook, Entwistle realised that Murray had a woman in tow. 'I said, "Where did that woman come from? I never noticed her in the pub." "Oh," Alby said, "we must have been making eyes at one another in the pub. I never noticed anything."'

Year		Aircraft		Pilot, or	2nd Pilot, Pupil	Duty
Month	Date	Type	No.	1st Pilot	or Passenger	(Including Results and Remarks)
—	—	—	—	—	—	Totals Brought Forward
MAY	3	LANCASTER III	G₂	SELF	F/O EMERSON	30TH. OPERATION
					SGT ENTWISTLE	SUPPLY DROPPING NEAR
					F/S MURRAY	ROTTERDAM 4 BLOCKS
					T/S FORD	OF 284 SACKS. 416 MLS
					F/S FREEZER	WEATHER STILL VERY
					F/S FIRKINS	SQUALLY

J. *Laurence* S/L
O.C. "C" FLIGHT

[signature] W/C.
C.O. 460 SQUADRON.

SUMMARY FOR. MAY.   TYPES.
UNIT   460 SQUADRON   LANCASTER I
DATE   5·5·45   LANCASTER III
SIGNATURE   *[signature]*

TOTAL HOURS FOR 460 SQUADRON.

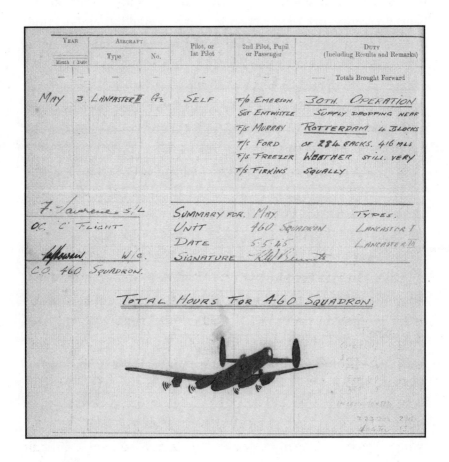

Chapter 6

First Time – Lucky?

No one could say they weren't scared. No one could
say that. You'd have to be, but you've got to wear it.

Alby Murray

IN 1945, A TOUR OF OPERATIONS for Lancaster crews amounted to
30 sorties. It was a count that at different times offered varying
chances of survival – albeit based on statistics. But the fact of the
matter was that any flight could be a crew's last, whether it was
their first or their thirtieth. Still, for anyone facing their first
mission, their apprehension must have been considerable. Hank
Nelson writes in *Chased by the Sun* that a survey of deaths-in-
action in 460 Squadron showed that 11 per cent were on their first
outing. This figure increased to 12 per cent on the third operation
when a crew was likely to carry out its first raid on a difficult
target. And of all deaths, 50 per cent occurred in the first six operations. However, by the sixth sortie, the rate fell dramatically to
3 per cent of all deaths and then to 2 per cent on the twentieth.

Of the crew, the pilot was the most likely to die because if the plane were shot and the crew forced to evacuate, the pilot would have to keep flying to keep the plane steady. Hence, he'd be the last to jump. (An exception of course was if the crew members were already dead or stuck in the confines of the kite with no means of escape.) This explains why the pilot was the one crew member who had his parachute with him at all times – in Bennett's case, he sat on it. The others had them nearby and within easy reach. A pilot's prospects of surviving the call to bail were not good. While the crew had an 8 per cent chance of survival, pilots had only 5 per cent. But in the case that anyone did survive a parachute drop, all crew wore Mae West inflatable life vests and were equipped with emergency kits that included used German bank notes, Benzedrine tablets to help crew speed up their actions as soon as they landed, chocolate and other concentrated foodstuffs, forged German food coupons, maps made of silk rather than paper to minimise noise when unfolding them while hidden, a compass, pictures of themselves in civilian clothes for forging documents, water purification tablets and, more often than not, a lucky charm.

It was not lost on crews that enemy flak or night fighters – or the danger of a mid-air collision with another Lancaster or a bomb from one above – were not their only dangers. Ironically, one of the Lancaster's greatest attributes – their massive 6350 kg bomb-load – was also their greatest danger. For even on take-off or during landing with bombs, the dangers of one or all exploding under the jostle and shake were very real. Each Lancaster also had a ground crew who held in their hands the lives of each crew member. For the job of ground crew was to refuel and maintain the Lancaster. The slightest error or haphazard task could cause a malfunction and lead to the most tragic of circumstances.

Ground crew – made up of armourers; electricians; instrument, engine and airframe fitters; spark-plug testers; radio mechanics – were often older than the flight crew. Many of them had families and were established workers in various trades whose skills were needed by the squadron. Ground crews took immense pride in their work and became as tightly bound as flight crews. Based in small and often hastily built huts located next to their Lancasters, these men often worked day and night in all manner of conditions to restore their kites. Even as crews carried out their operations, a member or two would remain on stand-by awaiting their return, ready to greet them with a cup of tea in one hand and a paintbrush in the other so they could 'brand' the Lancaster with the insignia of a bomb to mark another mission completed.

In postwar dispatches, the ground crew were regularly praised by their flight crew for their efficient work and dedication, especially for one of their riskiest and most difficult jobs. This was to fuse and load up a Lancaster with the selected bomb-load for an upcoming operation. This process was called 'bombing up' and would take hours to complete.

The breakdown of a bomb-load on a Lancaster varied, depending on the operation and target. There were four main bomb types that Lancasters carried:

- Magnesium incendiary: These were one of the most

destructive weapons, weighing 1.8 kg, loaded in large numbers and designed to create fires over a wide area.

- High-capacity 'Cookie': Weighed 1800 kg and relied on creating a maximum blast effect. With incendiaries, these were primary weapons in the bombing campaign.
- General purpose and medium-capacity bomb: High-explosive weapons that differed in weight-to-blast ratio. They came in larger sizes as the war progressed.
- Target indicator bombs: These needed to be accurately placed and highly visible. They released candles that burned in bright colours at predetermined heights above the ground.

However, on certain operations, Lancasters loaded up on other bomb types, such as mines that would be dropped at sea, or upgraded high-explosive bombs from 5400 kg 'Tallboys' to 10,000 kg 'Grand Slams'. With so many explosives, the process of 'bombing up' was never taken lightly. Indeed, they'd often be reminded of the dangers they faced.

One such occasion was the night of 3 July 1943 when a bomb-load was accidentally released from a Lancaster while sitting at the dispersal unit. As described in *Chased by the Sun*, the bombs and incendiaries exploded before they could be rolled away by ground crew, and the burning debris from the destroyed kite set alight the dispersal bay next to it. But with the danger of further planes and buildings meeting the same fate, the ground crew risked their lives to enter the two burning planes and shut off electrical systems and douse flames. Two Lancasters were destroyed and seven more made inoperable.

Nevertheless, the drama did not stop that night's bombing operation to Cologne.

~

Operation 1: Hanover, Friday 5 January 1945

Lost 39 kites. Plenty of fighters about! – Flight time (night): 5hrs 10mins

Keith Bennett's flight log entry

The first operation for any airman is a harrowing experience. 'The worst time is when you first see your name on the battle order,' recalls Cyril Entwistle. Possibly, it was toughest for the pilot in whose hands the rest of the crew's lives would rest. Well trained he might have been, and deemed fit to fly, but there was no certainty about how he would react in battle once they had broken through the German defence radar systems. No one could be sure of how a first-time pilot might react when under fire from the German 128 mm flak guns – or *Flugabwehrkanone* – or the more legendary 88 mm AA guns that could fire their 9 kg projectiles at a rate of 15–20 per minute and to a maximum range of 14,660 m at 45-degree angles. Or how he might react when under siege from a swarm of attacking twin-engine Junker JU 88s or Messerschmitt BF110 and 109 night fighters who were responsible for destroying 70 per cent of Lancasters. All this, while keeping his calm under pressure to find his way to the red markers dropped over the target zone by the preced-ing Pathfinders Force, which were matched by the green marks dropped by the operation master bomber that signalled all was set for the strike. Hence, first-time pilots like Bennett would take their first flight with another seasoned crew as 'second dickie', or second pilot.

For Bennett, this was in Lancaster X, skippered by Flying Officer Finlay on a night-time bombing mission to Hanover that, on a clear night, lasted 5 hours and 10 minutes. The importance of the pilot, while obvious, was never underestimated, especially by his crew who would fly with him after his hoped-for return from his operational baptism. In his logbook, Bennett noted the heavy flak they experienced, the large number of German fighters that greeted them, and the Allied losses – all with an exclamation mark, which would become typical of his style.

'Night-time flying must have been worse for Keith than any of us. At night there may be 700 or 800 of you, all at the target at the same time. There was a terrible danger of colliding,' says Entwistle, whose admiration for Bennett extended beyond the pilot's talent for handling the uncertain battle in the skies. Entwistle also admired Bennett's ability to deal with the exhausting monotony of flying in a Lancaster for hours on end when the enemy was out of sight but still lurked. 'God, the noise. The droning. Some nights we might have been flying for ten-and-a-half hours, which is a long time for Keith: watching instruments all the time, keeping on course and everything. The more deviation he made, the more work Les [Emmerson, the navigator] had to do. It was a long, tedious job. By the time you got back, perhaps over Holland, you begin to relax. All you want to do is shut your eyes and sleep. But to relax over Holland was one of the worst places because it was over Holland that a lot of damage was done.'

Operation 2: Merseburg, Sunday 14 January
Had to orbit target once. Never again. Flak heavier than Berlin. – Flight time (night): 8rs 20mins

As part of its continued Allied attack on Germany's oil plants, RAF Bomber Command committed 1100 aircraft to this night operation; it lost 14. The mission was a two-phased attack on the Leuna plant near Merseburg that followed an earlier attack at dusk on the German railways. The report in the London *Times* on 16 January 1945, headlined 'Big assault on enemy oil – plants and stores bombed – many fires at Leuna', explains how, simultaneously, a force of Halifaxes also bombed a fuel depot at Dulmen, near Munster, while Berlin also twice came under attack. And according to the newspaper, the bombing at the Leuna plant 'was well-orchestrated – in all, more than 2200 tonnes of bombs were dropped – and crews in the second attack reported that fires were burning in the target area when they arrived. They saw one very large explosion.'

For Bennett and his crew, flying into battle for the first time together was an intense experience. He recorded his reaction – as he had to – in his logbook, but in greater detail in a hastily written note found in his private collection of news clippings from the war:

Approaching heavily defended target was an awesome sight. Merseburg, a synthetic oil refinery centre, was said to have 1000 AA guns. The moonless night sky was a fireworks display of thousands of bursting shells. To pass through the barrage unscathed seemed impossible. But the German 88 mm guns – radar direction control was blanketed by 'window' – could not target selected aircraft except when individuals were out of the main stream.

Operation 3: Zeitz, Tuesday 16 January
Flak and searchlights/target. Mod. Heavy. – Flight time (night): 8hrs 10mins

Operation 4: Ludwigshafen, Thursday 1 February
Bags of flak and searchlights. Good prang [hit on target]. Clear break over target. 15 mins late.
– Flight time (night): 7hrs 15mins

Operation 5: Wiesbaden, Friday 2 February
Terrible weather conditions. 26 lost. – Flight time (night): 6hrs 35mins

Operation 6: Politz, Thursday 8 February
475 a/c. Lost 11. Most of trip in thick cloud. Sea leg to Denmark at 1500. Heavy scattered flak at Stettin. Bombed at 12,450 feet. A nerve racking trip. – Flight time (night): 8hrs 45mins

Bomber Command had 1000 aircraft in action on this night operation, according to the 10 February report in the London *Times*, which was titled 'Smashing blow at German oil – almost entire output believed inactive'. Again, the main target was a synthetic oil plant, this time at Politz, which was regarded as one of the two biggest such plants in Germany and specialised in aviation oil. It was subjected to two bombing attacks at two-hour intervals.

Earlier, Lancaster bombers with Mustang escorts from Bomber Command attacked two benzol plants in the Ruhr in daylight – the Robert Muser works outside of Bochum and the Ewald Fortsetzung works that were 5 kilometres northeast of Recklinghausen. Also that day, four railway marshalling yards that stood between the French border and Munich were attacked by 600 Liberators and Flying Fortresses and escort Mustangs and Thunderbolts from the US Air Force of which 19 bombers and three fighters were lost.

And even earlier, just before dawn, more Lancasters attacked a marshalling yard at Hojenbudberg, between Krefeld and Duisburg, while another raid by Halifaxes bombed a synthetic oil plant at Wanne-Eickel and Mosquito fighters swarmed on Berlin.

Operation 7: Dresden, Tuesday 13 February

Clear target. Bang-on bombing. Short of fuel. Couldn't make base. Landed Woodbridge. Dead beat. – Flight time (night): 9hrs 15mins

If there was one operation that Bennett rued during his tour, it was this mission over Dresden. To this day, it is still a topic of heated debate because of the death and destruction it caused. At the time, it was without a doubt 'one of the most powerful blows' – in the words of *The Times* newspaper – against German forces.

The Allies attacked the German army's vital communication centre in their war against the Russian armies of Marshal Konev that were fast approaching from the east. The combined load dropped on the city – also central to the rail network and German industry – was huge. In two attacks at night, Bomber Command committed 8000 aircraft out of its 14,000. In the first wave, 650,000 incendiaries with 3628 kg explosives and hundreds of 1814 kg cookies were dropped, creating one of the first-ever recorded firestorms where the fire was so intense that the updraft sucked up the air and oxygen as violently as a hurricane. In this case, where estimates reported a 20-square-kilometre area burnt to cinders, the phenomenon escalated when fresh winds fanned the fires.

The same night, Bomber Command executed attacks on the oil plant at Bohlen (south of Leipzig), Nuremberg, Bonn and Dortmund. The following day the US Air Force sent in 1350 heavy bombers and 900 fighters, many of them seeing the city ablaze from the previous night's raids. More raids were carried out over Chemnitz (65 km southwest of Dresden), Magdeburg, and Wessel.

The effectiveness of the raids cannot be disputed. *The Times* reported that the flak was light and passage over the bombing targets marked by the Pathfinders force was clear. The newspaper then quoted one Pathfinder pilot who said: 'There were fires everywhere, with a terrific concentration in the centre of the city.' And many pilots, according to the paper, later spoke of seeing smoke rise as high as 15,000 feet. Another pilot, one of the last to fly over the city that night, later recalled: 'There was a sea of fire ...The heat striking up from the furnace below could be felt in my cockpit ...The light inside the aircraft was that of an eerie autumn sunset. We were aghast at the awesome blaze. Although alone over the city, we flew around in a stand-off position.'

However, while the attack was lauded as a huge success by Allied commanders, and pivotal to eventual victory in the war, the deaths of so many people – most of them civilians – and the total obliteration of one of the most beautiful and architecturally rich cities in the world cannot be overlooked. In the aftermath of the war, there were conflicting reports of how many people exactly died among the population, which was 642,000 in 1939 and which by the time the raid was executed had increased by about 200,000 with an influx of refugees. The Nazis said that the mortality rate reached up to 250,000, while a more conservative figure was 25,000–30,000. Similarly, it is generally understood that many deaths were unaccounted for because of the numbers of uncounted people living in the city and because the firestorms caused by the bombing and subsequent winds burnt many people to cinders. Either way, the bombing of Dresden was still one of the greatest tragedies of the war. And Bennett, for the most part a taciturn man who remained tight-lipped about the war until his dying day, never spoke about his crew's role in the bombing that for them meant a near-ten-hour operation. But he did share with his wife and children his sorrow about the whole affair. The only written evidence of his sadness is the draft of a letter dated 3 December 1990 that he wrote to Jannie:

> It is a long time but when at a young age you have exceptional grim experiences as you had in WWII the memory always remains vividly with you . . . We all enjoyed the food-drops, such a relief after the bombings which I don't like to talk about. I wish now that it had never happened and I regret having taken part in the horrific mass destruction of Dresden and other historical cities.

The comments of Bennett's flight engineer, Cyril Entwistle – whose home city, Coventry, had been bombed to similar obliteration by the Germans – highlight the mixed messages many crews had received about the mission:

> All I knew about Dresden was Dresden china. We knew it was eastern Germany, but we didn't know much about the place . . . As I remember when we were briefed to go, they said: 'Well, the reason we're going is that Dresden is being flooded with refugees from the Eastern Front.' The Germans were only about 20 or 30 miles away. There is no way we can feed all these people, so we've got to discourage them from coming. That was as far as we knew. Psychology is psychology and the people who were in

front of the Russians on the Russian Front, all they could think of was to get away from the Russians because they were pretty well horrendous by all accounts.

'Henry' Ford says the first he knew of the devastation was via German radio: 'We didn't know anything about Dresden. I've heard people say: "You knew beforehand." But I never heard anybody protesting. Next thing I heard a German girl's broadcast. She's saying: "Butchers. This beautiful city, this heritage city, this innocent city of ancient craftworks of chinaware." We looked at each other [thinking] what the hell is going on? We didn't know the whole place had been engulfed by a fireball.'

Alby Murray was saddened by the operation: 'Dresden was a pity.' He says it was after the war that he and the crew fully understood the level of the devastation, saying, 'People started to talk about it in the press . . . their opinions. We couldn't do anything about it. You either go or if you don't they discharge you. If you give up, they say you lack moral fibre. They brand you.' Murray said the Dresden operation was billed as a 'morale-booster for the people' until 'they started to learn about it. I read one source that said 120,000 people were killed. I don't know whether that's correct. I'd say it'd be more like getting towards 150,000.'

Operation 8: Duisburg, Wednesday 21 February
Clear target. Lost S.I engine. 75 mins before bombing. Trailed by 2 ME 109s. – Flight time (night): 6hrs 30mins

Cyril Entwistle missed this flight because he accidentally returned to base from leave a day late and was later put on a 'milk run' – an unchallenged bomb run – with another crew under the command of Flight Lieutenant Stringer to Dresden. He quickly discovered that non-operational flights like these could be as dangerous:

Coming back over Denmark, the German fighters picked us up and they tailed us all the way back until we put our landing lights on to land at Binbrook. Then we started a rumpus. There were five from 460 Squadron on that, and twenty from two or three other squadrons. One of our navigators got hit in the leg, and another [plane] got shot down on the circuit, and another 29 were shot down in various aerodromes while out training. Apparently, the Germans put 147 fighters on that night and followed us. When we came back over the east coast they tucked in behind you and the radar didn't pick them up. We had strict radio silence. You couldn't warn anybody. I would have thought it would be better to break radio silence than allow all the Germans to come over here like that. I understand Flight Lieutenant Stringer and everybody else, had they reported these fighters, they probably would have been court martialled or something. That's the way things go. That was towards the end of the war as well.

First Time – Lucky?

Operation 9: Pforzheim, Monday 26 February
Bang on weather. Good prang. Good photograph – Jets up in force.
Flak light. – Flight time (night): 7hrs 55mins

Operation 10: Mannheim, Thursday 1 March
Flak moderate. Bombed. Wanganui cloud was 10/10. – Flight time
(day): 6hrs 55mins

Operation 11: Cologne, Friday 2 March
No log remarks – Flight time (day): 5hrs 30mins

This was another massive bombing attack involving 700
Lancasters and Halifaxes, but carried out in day-time and in
perfect early morning conditions. Nearly 3000 tonnes of bombs
were dropped in the first phase, the Deutz Bridge on the Rhine
being the main target. This was followed a few hours later by
another inundation of bombs, the principal target being about
800 metres from the Hohenzollern road and rail bridge, and
carried out by 180 more RAF heavy bombers that left all but the
city's cathedral in blazing ruins. The purpose of this operation
was to halt the Germans retreating from Cologne by blocking
their escape route west of the Rhine. According to one English
newspaper report, the intention was to make sure the aiming
points were 'so blocked with craters and rubble that movement
was impossible'. The same newspaper also quoted one
Canadian navigator who said: 'When the Yanks get to Cologne
they won't find much of it left.' As with most major operations,
others were carried out at the same time, luring the Luftwaffe

defence on several fronts, thus diverting their attention from Cologne. From the moment the sun rose at dawn to when it sank at dusk, fleet after fleet of Allied aircraft were reported crossing the Channel both ways. The Luftwaffe sent up its strongest fleet of aircraft in six weeks to 'welcome' the 1200 USAF Fortresses and Liberators that were escorted by 700 fighters and given the task of attacking various oil plants, tank factories, and rail yards in the areas surrounding Leipzig and Magdeburg. And it was the Luftwaffe that paid the highest price, losing up to 67 planes in the sky and another 36 on the ground, not to mention having exposed Cologne to the barrage of air attacks by Bomber Command. The operation was declared the 'finest yet' and 'probably the greatest day's air offensive of the war' by one British newspaper. The same report went on to say: 'The scale and tactics of the assault completely fooled the German defences. Berlin had an alert and warnings were sounded in scores of other towns because the bombers followed the route to the German capital and then swung suddenly to Dresden and Leipzig.'

Operation 12: Chemnitz, Monday 5 March
Easy target. Light flak – Flight time (night): 9hrs 30mins

Operation 13 (12a): Dessau, Wednesday 7 March
Too bloody near Berlin! Flak/fighters all the way to target. – Flight time (night): 9hrs 45mins

World War II airmen were a superstitious lot, evidenced by Bennett bracketing this thirteenth operation as number 12a. He also took with him on every flight a blue toy kangaroo named Joe that his mother had knitted; she would later embroider it with the name of each destination of his 20 operations. Alby Murray would take a call of nature on the port wheel of G2 before every flight. Cyril Entwistle was never without his packet of cigarettes: 'In case we went down in flames, I always said the last thing I would do is have one more fag.' Henry Ford would religiously wear a red ruby ring that his wife Pat had given to him – until he lost it in the fuselage of G2. Many airmen took with them copies of the Bible that their fathers had taken into battle in World War I, the books still encrusted with traces of mud from trench warfare. Others took family photos, St Christopher medals, lucky coins, or sprigs of wattle. One pilot made sure he wore muddied boots in every operation, simply because that's how he began his tour and his crew felt that if he cleaned them, it might change their fortune. Any airman needed luck to bail out of his plane and parachute to safety, a difficult feat that earned such airmen membership of the 'caterpillar' club – so named after the silk from caterpillars of which parachutes were made.

More than luck – closer to a blessing from above – was needed for an airman whose parachute failed to open after bailing out in freezing night-time conditions that could reach minus 60 Celsius, as happened to a friend of Entwistle's who was forced to jump from his shot-down Lancaster at about 800 feet during a night raid over Calais. 'His thumbs became so numb that he couldn't pull the release on his parachute,' recalls Entwistle. The airman, with two crew who had also bailed, spent the next three days hiding in shrubs by day to avoid being caught by the Germans, and tried by night to cross the enemy lines back into Allied hands. But Entwistle's mate failed to escape capture. He was caught by the Germans, whisked away in a plane to SS headquarters where he was greeted by an SS officer who spoke perfect English. 'He said, "Good afternoon, I'm sorry to see you in this predicament." Old Jack thought, "What a civilised bloke." Well, he'd been to Cambridge University. After that they got a rude awakening: they were shipped off. He spent three years as a POW.'

Operation 14: Kassel, Thursday 8 March
Good prang. Thin cloud. None lost. Flak intense at our height. One hole in M.U.G. turret fairing. – Flight time (night): 7hrs 05mins

Operation 15: Essen, Saturday 10 March
Good trip. Moderate flak. Accurate bombing through 10/10. Lost 3 out of 1000. – Flight time (day): 5hrs 20 mins

Operation 16: Dortmund, Sunday 11 March
Light heavy flak. Good trip. – Flight time (day): 5hrs 35mins

Dortmund was the second largest city to Cologne in the Ruhr on the region's eastern entrance. As a centre of communications, it was subjected to an attack by more than 1000 Lancasters and Halifaxes that formed a stream '100 miles long', according to

England's *The Daily Telegraph* newspaper. And again the newspaper billed it the 'biggest raid of the war'. As with Essen the
previous day, Dortmund was left in ruins, nothing but massive
smoke clouds rising from its centre. The attack, in which Polish
and Czech squadrons of RAF Fighter Command also participated, was scheduled for 4.30 pm with the aim of striking at the
southern end of Dortmund; it finally got underway at 5 pm.
And as with previous missions, the operation was preceded by
a day-time raid from USAF aircraft that included 1350
Fortresses and Liberators and 650 fighters – this time to the
Baltic port of Swinemunde, 60 km north of Stettin, to assist
the approaching Russian forces, and other marshalling yards
such as Seigen, Betzdorf, Dillenburg, Wetzlar, Friedburg and
Marburg.

Operation 17: Herne, Tuesday 13 March
*Heavy flak. Alby had very near miss. Front Perspex pierced. On G
attack a dead loss. – Flight time (night): 6hrs 10mins*

Every airman had a different way of handling the fear, but wireless operator Henry Ford's mutterings of potential doom and
gloom did little to settle the nerves of his fellow airmen on G2.
'He used to say: "I think we're going to cop it tonight,"' recalls
bomb-aimer Alby Murray. 'That's just what you need. I wanted
to job him one night. But it's all forgotten.'

Entwistle has not forgotten Ford's dark remarks, although
more than 60 years later he can openly laugh about them,
saying, 'Henry might have done it in jest sometimes. He'd say,

"We might not be here tomorrow." Even so, it got to you sometimes.'

Ford says his comments were only aimed at ensuring everyone was 'keeping on their toes' and alert. As he recalls, 'Keith always used to say, which is what a good leader should say, "Look, if you do everything right, as per the book, nothing can happen. It will be all right." Some of us used to say, "Yeah well, we can all do that, but it's still a matter of luck." You either had one attitude or the other, but there was still a lot of tension. Although, I did feel towards the finish that our luck had run out and we'd be lucky if we finished.'

Murray admits that one night he thought Ford's prophecy of gloom was about to come true – when he was struck in the hand by shrapnel while holding his two 303 guns in his front turret on the six-hour operation to Herne: 'On the anti-aircraft [guns], the missiles fragment when they reach their height . . . throw shrapnel everywhere. One came through the front on my perspex; hit me on the finger and made me bleed. That made me think.'

Other incidents also raised the suspicions of Bennett's crew, such as when they were 'coned' by the German searchlights and exposed as easy prey for the German night fighters or AA guns on the ground, lighting up the Lancaster's interior as clear as daylight. It was a terrifying and desperate moment for the crew, forcing them into a 'corkscrew', an evasive dive that would leave an airman's heart in his throat – but at least it offered a chance of escape. 'We weren't too keen on doing corkscrews,' says Ford, adding that there was always the danger of colliding with fellow bombers or escort planes, let alone being shot down. 'We were flying at 12,000 feet – there were other planes at 10,000, another at 11,000 or 8000 feet, and to corkscrew down through those, you're going to hit somebody surely, going very close. Your orientation is sort of limited as well.' It was a manoeuvre that required practice. The *g*-forces were horrendous, as one trial-run during an affiliation flight showed. When Bennett executed a 'corkscrew', the Perspex sky-light hatch above Ford in the wireless operator's seat was ripped off and threw Emmerson, who was sitting in the navigator's station, into chaos. 'Les was lying across his table, grabbing hold of his charts and pencils,' recalls Ford, laughing.

Firkins discovered first-hand the dangers of not being in position during a corkscrew when Bennett suddenly engaged in the manoeuvre while the rear-gunner was taking a natural break on the Elsan – the on-board chemical toilet that was, at best, loosely attached. But Firkins was not unaccustomed to such hazards. Once, when he failed to answer a call from Bennett, Ford found him with his strapping frame entangled with strips of ammunition. On another occasion, recalls Entwistle, Firkins accidentally set the rear turret alight by lighting up a cigarette during a flight, not realising that his oxygen tanks were leaking.

Operation 18: Misburg, Thursday 15 March
Oil plant near Hanover. Beautiful prang. 18,500 feet bombing height. – Flight time (night) 8hrs 00mins

Operation 19: Hanau, Sunday 18 March

No log remarks – Flight time (night): 7hrs 35mins

Operation 20: Gardening, near Heligoland, Wednesday 21 March

10 Lancs. Dropped 6 mines each. Error under 1 mile. A nice quiet trip. – Flight time (night): 4hrs 30mins

YEAR		AIRCRAFT		Pilot, or 1st Pilot	2nd Pilot, Pupil or Passenger	DUTY (Including Results and Remarks)
Month	Date	Type	No.			
—	—	—	—	—	—	Totals Brought Forward
May	3	Lancaster III	G₂	Self	F/O Emerson	30th Operation
					Sgt Entwistle	Supply dropping near
					F/S Murray	Rotterdam 4 blocks
					T/S Ford	of 284 sacks. 416 mls
					F/S Freezer	Weather still very
					F/S Firkins	squally

F. Lawrence S/L
O.C. 'C' Flight

_____ W/c.
C.O. 460 Squadron.

SUMMARY FOR. May
UNIT   460 Squadron
DATE   5.5.45
SIGNATURE RM Barnetts

TYPES.
Lancaster I
Lancaster III

<u>TOTAL HOURS FOR 460 SQUADRON.</u>

Chapter 7

The New Order

*Most of the Germans were not cruel, they were
common soldiers. Of course we disliked them
very much.*

Jannie Verstigen (née Van Splunder)

TO MAINTAIN COMMUNICATION with the Allies and the Dutch
government that was based in London during the war, the Dutch
listened to Radio Oranje which was broadcast through BBC
Radio from Stratton House in London. Meanwhile, the Dutch
Resistance had long set about organising a continuous campaign
of underground opposition to the Germans. Using a type B-Mark
II transmitter, the Resistance also co-ordinated its activities with
London and kept regular contact with the 21st Army in France,
Belgium, and the liberated regions of the Netherlands. They con-
ducted militia raids and clandestine dissemination of Allied-
sourced news published in *De Vliegende Hollander*, or *The Flying
Dutchman*. It was an Allied newspaper published in England in

Dutch that bore the British and United States flags on the masthead; its last edition came out on 10 May 1945 with the long-awaited and celebratory page-one splash headline of '*Duitschland Capituleert*'. Unsurprisingly, *The Flying Dutchman* was banned by the Germans, as were other anti-Nazi newspapers such as *Trouw* (Truth) and *de Vrije Pers* (The Free Press) which were brazenly published in Holland with a hand-operated stencil machine in Rotterdam. Four times a week, 10,000 copies of these papers came off the presses thanks to a team of five people, one of whom, Jo de Rek, was shot dead by the Germans in March 1945. Anyone caught reading or owning 'illegal' publications – let alone working for them – risked the punishment of death by firing squad. Hence the need for total secrecy in the publication and distribution of these journals. As such, they were often distributed by women who hid them in their babies' prams.

Despite the considerable risks, Jannie Van Splunder used to read *The Flying Dutchman* and she still has some copies today. Likewise, she risked writing her own diary which she kept buried for fear it would be discovered by the Germans. Each day she'd write about her fears, hopes, and the dramatic changes in day-to-day life under German occupation. Every night, she would sneak out and hide it in the hole she had dug. It became a source of strength for Jannie and helped her sustain her spirit. By the end of the war, the five volumes of her diary had become water damaged; consequently, she re-wrote every word of her secret thoughts. Today, where Jannie lives in the town of Hilversum, these diaries sit proudly and within easy reach in her living room.

Henri Arie Van Splunder, Jannie's father, was as daring during the war as she was. He too risked facing the firing squad. Despite his house being occupied by German troops, he continued to listen to Radio Oranje on a small wireless hidden in the piano in their living room. Miraculously, the Germans never detected or heard Henri's radio – though it must be said, they made things easy for him. As they stomped through the house in their thick leather boots, they gave Henri plenty of time to hide the radio before their approach.

As the famine continued to rage, Jannie could not help but suspect that some Germans enjoyed the suffering their occupation had brought upon the Dutch. One night, Jannie and her sisters, Rookje and Wilhelmina, discovered two German soldiers cooking sausages in their kitchen. 'We were crying because we were so hungry,' Jannie recalls. The Germans did offer them some sausage, but because they were the enemy the girls could not accept. Were the Germans teasing them, knowing their 'hosts' would be too proud to accept? Or were they being compassionate? Either way, their mother rewarded her three daughters for their resolve by giving each a cup of brown beans – then a rare commodity for the Dutch.

Meanwhile, the Germans became so comfortable at the Van Splunders' home that as room after room fell under their occupation, space became a premium for Jannie, her family, and her friend Bouwine who had been living with them since leaving her parents in Rotterdam. Eventually, the Van Splunder house was completely overtaken by German soldiers and for the last six weeks of the war, the family and Bouwine were forced to pack up their belongings and live in Jannie's father's nearby office in the town of Ridderkerk. Incredibly, Jannie was not filled with hatred for the Germans, as one might expect. But she certainly didn't like them. 'Most of the Germans were not cruel, they were common soldiers. Of course we disliked them very much.' Furthermore, Jannie knew that her family's experience was not unique; sacrifice and risk-taking were commonplace right across Europe.

Jannie's husband-to-be, Gerrit Verstigen – whom she met just after the Allied liberation – was such a case in point. Like so many Dutchmen whom the Germans regarded as fit, strong and able-bodied, he was taken away from his home in Rotterdam early in the occupation and sent by train to a forced labour camp in Germany. However, during the journey, Gerrit managed to escape from the train and hid in a small village north of Amsterdam until the last year of the war. By this time he had joined the Dutch Resistance and had returned to Rotterdam for his assignment. He was to pretend that he was an artist, painting and drawing panoramic harbour views, but his artworks would conceal secret etchings of German military build-ups and movements which would be dispatched to the underground. Like all undercover Resistance missions, he risked immediate death if caught. And while the handgun he always carried would hardly help to avoid arrest, it might enable him to take down a few enemies in the process.

The fear of losing family who worked with the Resistance

was ever-present for Henk Benness. His father and uncle were both enlisted, and for security reasons had code names. His uncle was a group leader in the underground while his father worked in administration, keeping track of night-time weapon deliveries from the Allies. 'The weapon-drops were very, very risky. Holland is a small country and the planes, like a DC3 which sometimes brought agents with them, often had to land in small meadows,' explains Benness. During these delivery runs, his father and his colleagues had to alert incoming planes that it was OK to land by first lighting a torch, then by igniting a string of small fires that would outline the impromptu runway on which they could land.

'They would land, drop everything and then they would be off again. They then had to hide the weapons, mainly Sten guns, in farms. My uncle would meet there and plan raids.

'It was very risky. If they [Germans] caught you they shot you on the spot. The German army was not that bad, but the SS, they were real bastards. They were real fanatics.'

The Resistance was an effective force that complemented the wave of Allied attacks on German installations in western Holland. The Allies bombed railway lines and trains that transported food, supplies and personnel to and from Germany; Dutch ports which held German battleships and U-boats; and launching sites for the German V-2 pilotless bombers that were sent off to attack London. Sadly and unavoidably, many of those bombings cost Dutch lives, such as the bombing of the V-2 site near The Hague in March 1945 where the target was missed due to a navigation error and civilian households were struck instead, causing the deaths of up to 2000 people.

While the Resistance was a key element in the battle for final liberation of western Holland, their actions were not without retribution. As payback for their raids, the Germans executed groups of innocent Dutch civilians where German facilities had been destroyed, Dutch worker enlistment destabilised, or enemy forces killed.

In February 1943, the Germans acted swiftly after a Resistance cell shot and killed Dutch collaborator Hendrik A. Seyffardt in The Hague. Resistance fighters rang his doorbell and after he answered and confirmed his identity, they shot him twice in the stomach. The next day, his death resulted in the execution of 50 Dutch civilians and raids on Dutch universities.

One of the greatest atrocities committed by the Germans as retribution for the Resistance's action came on 30 September 1944 after an ambush of four German soldiers near the village of Putten went horribly wrong. Only one of the Germans was taken hostage, as three of them managed to escape and raised the alert. The response was swift and brutal: the German general commander of the area, General Heinz Helmuth von Wuhlisch, put out the order for all the inhabitants of Putten to be arrested and for Putten to be razed. In a bid to save them, the Resistance decided to let their hostage go, but it was too late. The Germans rounded up every male in the village and transported all 589 of them to working camps in Germany. By the end of the war, only 49 of those men had survived. As for the estimated 600 houses in Putten that were to be burned down, fortunately the number destroyed was limited to 87.

But by no means was the incident an isolated one. The assassination on 23 October 1944 of SD officer Herbert Oelschagel in Amsterdam by the Resistance drove the Nazis to arrest 29 civilians the following day, then at gunpoint forcing local pedestrians on the Appollolaan to watch their execution by firing squad. The Nazis also set fire to a number of buildings, leaving them to burn down.

An even more grisly and blood-curdling outcome followed another night-time raid by the Resistance on 6 March 1945. The Resistance had planned to ambush and steal a German lorry, but instead they shot up a BMW car, seriously injuring its high-ranking passenger, SS General Hans Albin Rauter, and killing his driver and orderly. Rauter, taken to hospital, survived the raid after receiving a number of emergency blood transfusions, but there were heavy reprisals for the incident, mercilessly carried out by the ruthless SD – the Sicherheitsdienst, or intelligence service of the SS formed in 1931. Under the orders of SS Brigadeführer Dr Eberhardt Schongarth, 116 local Dutch men were rounded up, taken to the scene of the ambush, shot dead and then buried in a mass grave in Heidof Cemetery. Furthermore, a number of Dutch prisoners in Gestapo camps throughout the occupied Netherlands were also randomly picked and executed by firing squad as part of the payback for the ambush.

In this case, there was at least eventual retribution for what was regarded as one of the gravest wartime atrocities committed by the Germans on Dutch soil. Rauter was arrested by the British Military Police and later tried by a Dutch court, which found him guilty. He was condemned to death by hanging. Schongarth met the same fate. Tried by a British military court, he was hanged in 1946.

A major task carried out by the Resistance, who operated in small cell groups, was the underground movement of people – whether they were refugees, escaped Allied prisoners of war, or captured Germans who would be put into Allied hands – to liberated regions of the Netherlands. And it was through the rugged Biesbos National Park that these *onderduikers* – as they collectively became known – commonly made their escape to freedom and safety. The Biesbos, southeast of Rotterdam, is full of rivers, peat, moors, islands, and strong tide activity, all of which provided the Resistance with the ideal access channel to reach Dutch territory already rid of Nazi rule. The Biesbos was also a perfect hiding place for the Resistance, or anyone on the run from the Germans. The enemy's knowledge of the area and its tidal patterns was far inferior to that of the Dutch, especially the local people, many of whom knew every nook and cranny in the park.

The Biesbos had eight secret routes into the liberated region of the Netherlands which the Resistance took in the thick of night by row-boat, or later by motor-launch provided by the Canadian army. Besides the transport of people, the Resistance used the routes to secretly deliver urgently needed medicine and supplies that saved many lives during a period when thousands of people were dying every day.

One route was for the passage of captured German prisoners who were detained en masse – up to 75 men – in a secret camp created for them at the hidden departure point. It was manned from mid-1944 by a group of Dutch who had been hiding from the Germans; this group also raided rationing offices where food and supply coupons were kept, and confiscated weapons and supplies from the Germans for their own use. Two routes were dedicated solely to Allied prisoners of war who had escaped from various camps; another route was used for the transfer of Allied pilots who had been shot down, spies, couriers, and anyone wanted by the Germans; while a fifth was used only by the Resistance. Of the three other routes, one was an emergency back-up should a problem occur with access to any of the other routes, while the remaining two were simply alternative routes that had access points from various villages that could be quicker to reach if necessary.

Rotterdam and Amsterdam had suffered immeasurably. Compounding the lack of food and the general brutality of German occupation was the enemy's fervent push to deport the Jewish population to death and labour camps. In Amsterdam, where the Gestapo was based, Jews were forced to live in ghettos and forbidden entry to many public facilities. They were compelled to wear yellow Stars of David, and it wasn't long before the deportations began.

But the move to rid the city of a Jewish population met resistance from the Dutch communists who were rich in number in Amsterdam. Until this point, the Nazis had faced little opposition to their treatment of the Jews – although it had not yet reached the levels of barbarity that it ultimately would. Initially, the communists expressed their opposition to the Nazis' anti-Jewish policies via illegal pamphlets which were distributed by the underground. But then in February 1941, when a group of Jews was transported to a concentration camp in Mauthausen, they ramped up their opposition. The communists took the unprecedented step of calling for a nationwide workers' strike to protest against the deportation. This was the first such action in Nazi-occupied Europe. Unfortunately, the protest didn't have much impact for the strike-call only incensed the Germans whose anti-Semitic actions intensified. As Jews were rounded up for transportation, many were publicly humiliated, beaten, or even executed on the spot.

In Rotterdam, the Jews were called up to report for work camps in July and August of 1942. They were told to assemble at 'Shed 24', a shed on the southeastern docklands of Rotterdam; from there they were transported by train to camps across occupied Europe. Shed 24 no longer exists, but in its place is a grassed block of land that sits in the shadows of drab, towering apartment blocks. A small sign saying 'Shed 24' is the simple but powerful commemoration of what the site signifies for Rotterdam's past.

Following that initial order, in September 1942 the Germans took a new approach to the call-up. The plan was to identify all Jewish residents of Rotterdam who had originated from Germany and eastern Europe, and transport them to labour and extermination camps. Many first went to transit camps such as Westerbroek, near Groningen, in the northeast of the country; or to work camps at Vuught in central Holland; and Amersfoort, southeast of Amsterdam. On 8 October 1942, all Jews with German and eastern European origin aged between 69 and 90 years were transported. Then on 15 October, those women and children whose husbands and fathers had been deported were made to follow the same fate. Those among them who had continued to ignore the order to report to the 'Shed 24' meeting point were arrested in their homes. Then came the next phase of the Jewish round-up. In February 1943, residents of the Jewish old people's homes and Jewish Hospital – and anyone who worked there – were arrested and deported to extermination camps in Germany.

In the aftermath of the war, it was estimated that of the 140,000-strong Jewish population who lived in the Netherlands, only 30,000 survived. Ironically, the efficiency of Dutch records, which made it easy for the Germans to identify and arrest Jews, contributed to the high death-toll. Furthermore, the country's topography made it easy for the Nazis to capture any Jews who tried to escape as the flat wastelands made hiding extremely difficult. Many Jews did hide in other people's homes – such as Anne Frank, whose daily diary became a worldwide best-seller when published after the war – however, many were ultimately caught and either died in camps – like Frank – or were executed, alongside those people who were courageous enough to hide them.

German ruthlessness was not confined to eliminating the Jews, counterattacking the Resistance and brutalising the Dutch. In what later became known as the Texel Massacre, the Nazis showed they could be just as merciless in combating any force that attempted to oppose them – even from within.

In late April 1945, the German forces on the island of Texel faced a mutiny from its 800-strong Russian contingent. Known as the 822nd infantry battalion, the contingent was led by 400 German officers and NCOs (non-commissioned officers) and was manned by Russians who had been taken prisoner and volunteered to fight on the German side.

One night the Russians snuck into the Germans' quarters and succeeded in killing 250 of them. The Germans responded with characteristic swiftness: Nazi command on the mainland ordered troops to Texel and the island was brought back under German control. The Russian rebels were arrested and punished, and a total of 565 Russians were killed, as well as 117 local Dutch from Texel.

YEAR		AIRCRAFT		Pilot, or 1st Pilot	2nd Pilot, Pupil or Passenger	DUTY (Including Results and Remarks)
Month	Date	Type	No.			
—	—	—	—			—— Totals Brought Forward
MAY	3	LANCASTER III	G²	SELF	F/O EMERSON	30TH. OPERATION
					SGT ENTWISTLE	SUPPLY DROPPING NEAR
					F/S MURRAY	ROTTERDAM. 4 BLOCKS
					F/S FORD	OF 284 SACKS. 416 MLS
					F/S FREEZER	WEATHER STILL VERY
					F/S FIRKINS	SQUALLY

F. Lawrence S/L
O.C. 'C' FLIGHT

[signature] W/c.
C.O. 460 SQUADRON.

SUMMARY FOR. MAY.
UNIT   460 SQUADRON
DATE   5·5·45
SIGNATURE   [signature]

TYPES.
LANCASTER I
LANCASTER III

TOTAL HOURS FOR 460 SQUADRON.

Chapter 8

The Run Home

*We were a fairly irreverent crew, but I couldn't help
feeling that some guiding hand had been helping us.*

Peter Firkins

Operation 21: Bremen, Friday March 23

*Bang-on day. Flak intense. Hit on bombing run. Lost stb outer and
lots of fuel. Made for nearest suitable drome in England. Landed at
Hethel near Norwich on 2 engines. Stb. inner feathered. A fuel line
was cut. Both pitch levers on stb. Cut. Only 9 holes in a/c [aircraft]. –
Flight time (day): 4hrs 40mins*

BENNETT AND HIS CREW were given a hint that this daylight operation would be different when they were suddenly woken up at 3 am by the Service Police. They were ordered to report for the traditional pre-op breakfast of bacon and eggs and attend an official operation briefing. They were told their target would be

123

the bridge at Bremen – a key supply-line to German ground forces. That they were to fly came as a total shock. Their squadron had not received a battle order the day before, so they were looking forward to a day off. Seizing the opportunity to let off some steam, they'd spent the evening drinking together at the popular Black Swan hotel – aka the 'Mucky Duck' – at Grimsby.

Still, despite their shock and lack of mental preparation, all seemed to go as usual for Bennett and his crew on G2 as they took off just before dawn. They didn't come under attack on the way and Bennett's G2 flew steadily towards the target in sunny conditions. But suddenly, nearing Bremen and the bridge they were to bomb, all hell broke loose, as rear-gunner Firkins recalls in *Heroes Have Wings*: 'Hundreds of grey-black clouds of smoke appeared in the sky as we began our run up to the Pathfinders' markers. The smell of cordite filled our nostrils as flak burst all around.'

The flak was typically insistent. And after Murray dropped the G2's load of thirteen 1000 lb (454 kg) and four 500 lb (226 kg) bombs, they were suddenly struck under the starboard wing, the hit severing their starboard fuel-lines and tanks. Recalls Firkins: 'I heard Bennett who had a somewhat bucolic air but was in fact a brilliant pilot yell, "Christ, my arse is on fire!" And I saw what I believed to be white smoke pouring past my rear turret. Actually it was petrol, 400 gallons of it, vaporising in the cold air of our bombing height of 15,000 feet.' Quickly, Bennett discovered that he had lost two starboard engines, and as fuel continued to spew out – with the fumes filling the cabin air –

the situation was looking grim for all. Making it worse, the red distress flares fired by the crew and intended to attract the support of Allied fighter planes were ignored, largely due to their own preoccupation with a solid defence of Luftwaffe aircraft. 'We were in deep trouble,' says Firkins.

Left to their own devices, Bennett, flight engineer Cyril Entwistle, and navigator Les Emmerson set about working out a strategy. They decided to fly to the Dutch coast, attempt to cross the Channel and still land in England, despite fuel running low.

As G2 and several other lame Lancasters flew back together, thinking that safety in numbers offered a better chance of survival against any marauding German fighters, Firkins could not help but take in the surreal view from the rear turret: 'I could see many thrilling dogfights as Luftwaffe and Allied fighters battled on in the beautiful spring morning.'

By the time G2 reached the coast, they had dropped from 15,000 to 4000 and then to 2000 feet, but they remained committed to a Channel attempt rather than land in enemy territory and risk being taken prisoner.

The crossing was a stroke of genius that was as much a measure of Entwistle's power of mind as it was of Bennett's skill and calm under pressure. After the war he was awarded the Distinguished Flying Medal (DFM) on Bennett's recommendation.

It's little wonder that Bennett was impressed by his English crewmate. Entwistle had to calculate exactly how much fuel they had left and how much longer they could fly on it.

And he measured it to G2's last roll of the wheel. For soon after crossing the Channel and following Emmerson's call to fly to the nearest airstrip – the US base at Hethel – Entwistle realised that their fuel supply was close to dry. Then, as Hethel came into view and the G2 came down to about 100 feet, he calmly informed Bennett in his soft Yorkshire brogue, 'We're out of fuel, skipper – you'll have to go straight in.' As Bennett prepared to land, the two port engines drained the remaining fuel supply. Then he glided in for a three-point landing, the engines cutting out altogether as he did so.

The dramatic landing certainly awoke the US base, which immediately dispatched their emergency services to come to the aid of the wounded G2. The runway was immediately swamped with a convoy of speeding fire-engines, ambulances and jeeps in hot pursuit of G2 until it came to a final halt. Firkins never forgot the stunned look of one US officer and his words to Bennett: 'Say, you orta [sic] get a goddamned DFC for this.'

'We were a fairly irreverent crew, but I couldn't help feeling that some guiding hand had been helping us during the longest and slowest two-and-a-half hours of our lives,' recalls Firkins. The crew were flown back to Binbrook the next morning.

Two nights later, Bennett and his crew couldn't help but wonder whether they were pushing their good fortune. Flying a new aircraft as theirs was being repaired, they were faced with yet another drama as they were taxiing out onto the runway in the early evening when visibility was difficult. Firkins, in the rear turret, was in the prime position to witness what unfolded and nearly cost him his life. As he recalls:

We were just turning onto the perimeter track when I glimpsed a Lancaster bearing down on us. Its two port engines were coming into line somewhere about the position of my rear turret. I yelled 'Look out!' over the intercom and with visions of two full bomb-loads going up, I swung my turret to the beam, to line up the doors in order to beat a hasty retreat. But I jammed my rather bulky frame in the small turret door just as the two aircraft came to a grinding halt, with the port propellers of the other aircraft chopping through our fuselage a few feet from my turret.

For Bennett in the pilot seat, there was no doubt about the potential horror that awaited him from behind. Failing to get Firkins on the intercom and fearing the worst – that Firkins would be incinerated – he scrambled through the escape hatch and ran down the top of the fuselage towards the rear turret. In the meantime, Entwistle had shut off all the electricity and power to minimise the fire risk. To say Bennett was relieved to find Firkins very much alive and not seriously injured – just stuck in the turret door – was an understatement. A further miracle was that the plane did not burn up. 'Why we didn't set on fire, I don't know,' says Henry Ford.

However, the incident was not without ramifications, especially since the pilot of the other Lancaster was the Flight Commander. There was an immediate inquiry into the matter, with Bennett having to answer what were believed to be allegations of blame. Entwistle also recalls the accusatory Flight

Commander submitting as evidence the fact that his vision had been impaired because the tail-lights on Bennett's plane were not on. But as Entwistle clarified, this was after the collision, and due to the fact that he had cut the electricity for safety reasons. Bennett's crew knew who should carry the blame, and it was not their skipper who, they felt, had been unfairly scapegoated because he was the junior officer. They met in private, and without Bennett's knowledge, planned his defence. They submitted a written account of the incident to their superiors who were conducting the investigation.

But as the dust settled on what would have been their thirteenth operation in 24 days, the thought of what may have happened had they taken off and flown their mission to Hanover emerged. 'We were all pretty tired, though we did not realise it at the time, and we were disposed to feel that fate had once again played a part in our destinies. We felt that, if the collision had not prevented us from flying, we would almost certainly have "bought it" during the operation that night,' says Firkins.

If there was some good to come from the accident apart from it forcing them to avoid an 'unlucky' 13th operation in 24 days, it was that Bennett and his crew managed to get some time off while their Lancaster was repaired. And as Bennett's diary shows, it didn't take long for him to cast aside the horrors of the war and readjust to the pace of village life. As with most airmen, Bennett made the best of his free time – always living with the possibility that his next operation could well be his last.

The Run Home

Monday, 26 March

Beautiful day. Warm, sunny like spring at home. No ops on. Wrote home. Jeanne and Mrs Edmonds. Monty's 2-day offensive going OK.

Tuesday, 27 March

Another grand day – a battle order out but was not on. Getting ready for leave. Wrote home. Jeanne and Mrs Edmonds.

Wednesday, 28 March

Battle order out early but has been put off. Weather dull. Left for London. Noticed interesting old castle when passed through Tealby [village in Lincolnshire]. Arrived at Boomerang club at 6.00. Had some ice-cream and saw a show. Jimmy Durante in Music for Millions – bang on show. Met Bert Wright. Big advances today, reckon war will be over in a few weeks.

Thursday, 29 March

No joy from Taylor. Met Mac from Quinty and Ted Jacobs. Saw two shows today. 'Great Day' at the Playhouse and Tommy Trinder in 'Happy and Glorious' at the Palladium. Bang on show. Rang Auntie Lil.

Friday, 30 March

Up early to catch 8.40 at Euston to Coventry. Met Cyril and his mother and his girlfriend Dorothy. After tea travelled to Birmingham by bus. Arrived at Auntie Lil's home at 8.30. Had some more tea and visited Red Lion. Visited Alfred Horboat's with Cyril. Very interesting. War going well.

Saturday, 31 March

Got up at 12 noon and got ready for a wedding. Travelled in Ted's car with Uncle Bill to Aycliffe. Had a couple of grogs at the Squirrel and walked to Highcliff on the other side of the Swan. Both mining towns. A real mining wedding and we all had a good party after the supper. Met Barbara. Was home about 12ish.

Sunday, 1 April

Rose brightly at noon and went out at 3 to visit Uncle Harold with Jill and Auntie. He was very pleased to meet us. His wife's name is Maude and the two children are Maureen 10 and Alan 3. Irelen, 20, is adopted by Aunt Nellie. Left after a supper of two eggs at 8.30.

With it likely that another operation was approaching, Bennett would have considered the fact that he was nearing the back-end of his tour. All airmen did, as they counted down their 'ops' to the magical 30 mark that at this time of the war was the amount required to register a full tour. Although, while the end may have been in sight, those last operations were also the most potentially hazardous for Bennett and his crew, for it was during such missions when aircrew, thinking of home and excited by the prospect of an imminent return, could subconsciously drop their guard and pay the price for it by either exposing their Lancaster to attack from the ground or by the Luftwaffe night fighters; or inadvertently losing their place within the bombing stream and colliding with another bomber; or accidentally flying into the path of a falling bomb that had been released from a plane above.

The danger of heightened complacency was also exacerbated by the pendulum of domination of the war, now swinging back in favour of the Allies, as the Germans had been forced into retreat and were under siege, in large part due to the bombing raids carried out by Bomber Command, 460 Squadron and Bennett's crew.

Operation 22: Lutzkendorf, Wednesday 4 April
Oil plant near Leipzig. Good prang; photo plotted in small target area. Landed on 3 in bad conditions. Light flak searchlights. – Flight time (night): 8hrs 25mins

Operation 23: Kiel, Monday 9 April
Clear target. Good prang. Bags of flak, rockets, searchlights, few Jerries. Admiral Scheer sunk. – Flight time (night): 5hrs 40mins

The sinking of the *Admiral Scheer* while in dock at Kiel in the Baltic was an important strike for Bomber Command, especially as this was not the first attempt. On 4 September 1939, the ship – regarded against convention by the Allies as 'male' – was hit by three bombs dropped by Bristol Blenheims, but sustained only minor damage.

The *Admiral Scheer*'s first mission was in July 1936 to evacuate German civilians from the civil war in Spain, while in May 1937 'he' was used to shell Almeria in Spain. But in 1940, the *Admiral Scheer* was re-classified from an armoured ship – or *Panzerschiff* – to a heavy cruiser. However, the Allies regarded him as a 'pocket battleship'.

At 14,000 tonnes, his weight exceeded the maximum of 10,000 tonnes for such a boat under international law as outlined in the Versailles Treaty. The *Admiral Scheer* was also equipped with six 11-inch guns and, under his diesel-powered engines, reached a maximum speed of 26 knots. He played a significant role in escalating the battle for naval superiority during the war, as the boat's breach of international limits spurred a domino effect with countries on both sides competing to outdo each other in boat size and naval capacity.

The operation to sink the *Admiral Scheer* cost Bomber Command ten planes.

Operation 24: Kiel Bay Mining, Friday 13 April

Laid 6 mines. Error under 3mls. None lost. Moderate light flak. A good trip. – Flight time (night): 6hrs 00mins

Operation 25: Heligoland, Wednesday 18 April

Bang on and accurate bombing. Lost escort 13 sqdns Mustangs, 10 of Spits. – Flight time (day): 4hrs 20mins

Saturday, 21 April

Was woken up at 4.15. Briefing at 5.15. Target was to be Berchtesgaden but the op was scrubbed. Hope we go there soon. Am standing by again for another early morning call. What a life! Terrible show at cinema – more dance band type shows. War's still being won! It seems today was Hitler's birthday – that accounts for the special raid – pity we didn't go.

Operation 26: Bremen, Sunday 22 April
Brought the bombs back after getting to target. Slight flak. Carried a cookie. 8 × 1000, 4 × 500. Good day. 7/10 cloud over. Target only 1½ mls from Monty's 2nd Army. – Flight time (day): 4hrs 40mins

Sunnday, 22 April
Standing by for ops in morning. Took off after lunch for Bremen. Cloud most of the way and 1/10 over had to bring bombs back. Monty wants this target bashed especially. British 2nd Army only 1½ miles away. Joe will be king of Berlin soon.

Monday, 23 April
A cool day spent fiddling about with log-book. Joe in Berlin suburbs. Should meet Americans very soon. Airletter from Mum and Jeanne. Blackout lifted from today.

Tuesday, 24 April
Bang on day, nothing down in the way of ops. Flew on fighter affil. This afternoon, u/s [unserviceable] the G etc but couldn't shake off the fighter. He was pretty good. Did a bit of low flying over sea. Went to pictures to see not too bad a show. On battle for tomorrow. Joe is in Berlin now.

Operation 27: Berchtesgaden, Wednesday 25 April
Cookie hung up. Had to land with it on. Got an aiming point photo. Flak intense at times. – Flight time (day): 8hrs 20mins

Days of anticipating a role in one of the most important missions in the war came to an end for Bennett and his crew when they took off at 5 am – significantly – on Anzac Day. Along with the twenty Lancaster bomber crews from 460 Squadron, this would be their last attack of the war. Their target was Adolf Hitler's chalet retreat known as 'The Eagle's Nest' at 1835m altitude on the Obersalzburg in the northern sector of the Swiss Bavarian Alps, 28 kilometres from the town of Berchtesgaden. Also targeted for bombing was Hitler's other and more utilised retreat on the same mountain but just below 'The Eagle's Nest' – the Berghof or *Haus Wachenfeld* – as well as the SS barracks.

As Allied bombers and RAF and USAF Mustang escort fighters set off, on land General Patton's Third Army was within 120 kilometres of the target zone. Meanwhile, German ground forces on the other side of the Alps in Italy were retreating. Cyril Entwistle can still recall the surreal atmosphere as they flew to their target:

I often thought when we went to Berchtesgaden – it was a lovely day, hardly a cloud around, and we were rumbling right across sleepy little villages here and there – and I thought, even at the time, 'We are putting the fear of God into all these people. They know bloody well we are all laden with bombs. It is a lovely peaceful day like this and we're going to cause havoc to these people.' There'd been no alert [for the attack] for about four days before that, to go to Berchtesgaden. Word came through each time saying Hitler wasn't there, and so they waited until such time until they were certain that he was there.

Hitler was not at either of the two locations, but in his Berlin bunker. However, the operation was nevertheless deemed a huge success even though 'The Eagle's Nest' survived the attacks, as the other targets were seriously damaged by the drops that included 12,000 lb (5443 kg) bombs designed for enhanced target penetration. Photos of the destruction made page-one of English newspapers when they were published on 20 May. 'What we did to Hitler's home' was the headline in the *Sunday Dispatch* above a picture of Hitler's shattered Berghof chalet; a second showed the interior devastation of the German Führer's favourite living room from where he had a clear view across the pristine Swiss Alps. The *Sunday Express* ran the headline: 'Hitler wouldn't know the old chalet-home now' above two more pictures, again showing the exterior and interior impact of the bombing raid.

Bennett was eager to participate, as is clear from his log and diary entries on the day and those preceding it. His remarks were echoed by many airmen who took part, such as those quoted in *The Daily Sketch* newspaper on 26 April: 'This is the target I have been waiting for all the war,' Flight Lieutenant and navigator E.F.A. Jones from Newcastle-on-Tyne was reported as saying. 'There was a really good concentration of bombs. I was really glad to see SS barracks take a heavy beating.' The paper also quoted Flight Sergeant E.J. Cutting, a rear-gunner from Lingwood: 'I saw one terrific flash right on Hitler's house. It was a 12,000-pounder all right.'

Bennett and his crew came close to becoming part of this 'terrific flash' on this, their last operation. Upwind, on the edge of smoke and from a height of 5486 metres (18,000 feet), they managed to drop their four 453 kg bombs, one 226 kg bomb and a 113 kg bomb. But their biggest bomb, a 1814 kg 'cookie', failed to drop. It became stuck – or 'hung up' – in the bomb bay and Bennett was forced to return to England for a 1.30 pm landing at Binbrook. With the bomb still in the bomb bay, such a manoeuvre was highly risky as should landing be rough, the bomb would dislodge and explode. Entwistle recalls:

> We tried to get rid of it several times and it just wouldn't go. On one occasion I'd been back, lifted the floorboard where the bomb station and cookie was. I took a screwdriver down – now what happens, when the bomb-aimer presses the release, the electric circuit goes between and the solenoid opens these hooks and they drop down to release the bomb. We thought at first, perhaps it's frozen up. So I went back, got the screwdriver and got Alby to press the bomb release and I prised the solenoid hook out. I nearly had a fit, I did. The release stick, it went back. There was 4000 pounds hanging down there on one hook! I was in a bit of sweat there. So I put the floorboards back and we left it. Keith then landed and didn't report it. He got pulled over the coals for that. He got a damn hot 'in future, let people know about it'.

In Entwistle's opinion, if Bennett deserved anything, it was the decoration of a 'Bar' for his safe landing rather than a reprimand. Henry Ford concurs about Bennett's landing ability:

'He always prided himself on doing a good land, especially the one after Berchtesgaden.' And Ford has no doubt about the inherent dangers of trying to land safely with a 'cookie' hung up: 'Other planes landed, only to see the cookie chasing them down the runway, skidding after them because they'd come loose from the jolt of the landing.'

The incident was mentioned in the official 460 Squadron post-operation report about the raid on Berchtesgaden. Marked 'secret', it reads:

Twenty aircraft were detailed to operate against the above target. There was no cloud and visibility was good. The group maintained fair formation and correct height until about 4 degrees east, when two separate gaggles formed. The leaders leading the rear gaggle. They fired yellow lights at 6 degrees east and half of the group formed up into a reasonable column, but at least 80 aircraft were ahead of the leaders and made no effort to come back. At turning point 0900 degree east, some of these aircraft orbited and came into the column but there were still many stragglers and as leaders were flying south of the track, the column was not good. The track made good almost eliminated the turning point at 12 degrees east and the last turn to the target was made at least 10 miles wide. The lake on the approach to the target not being sighted by the leading aircraft. The Master Bomber had difficulty in locating the target and eventually turned to port where the target was located and marked with reds. This meant that nearly all the leading aircraft of the column had to orbit. Some aircraft turning as far as Salzburg where they were engaged by heavy, moderate barrage flak. Bombing developed well, initial stages at starboard of A/P. Master Bomber called main force over to bomb to port and the whole target area was then well covered, Master Bomber giving general instructions on 'Pickwick'. Owing to leaders orbiting the target, column was a hopeless scramble and the main force was lucky not to have been intercepted by fighters at this stage. One of our aircraft failed to return – 'M' NX 585 F/O Payne – no news since take-off. The following bomb-load was carried by the squadron: 20 × 4,000 lb bombs, 80 × 1000 lb bombs, 20 × 500 lb bombs and 20 × 250 lb bombs. Bomb or incendiary load carried by aircraft on abortive sorties – nil. Bombs or incendiaries brought back as a result of technical failure to release – 1 × 4000 lb bombs [that being Bennett's cookie]. Bombs and incendiaries jettisoned – nil.

One of the twenty crews who took part in this last bombing raid for 460 Squadron did not return, indicating that despite the odds, statistics, or even crew-record of a bomber crew, such a prospect was a constant. For those who returned to Binbrook from Berchtesgaden, the loss highlighted their reliance on 'Lady Luck'.

Bennett's rear-gunner Peter Firkins gives an account of a narrow escape in his book *Strike and Return*. He describes the experience of Flying Officer H.D. 'Lofty' Payne who was flying in his seventh operation when his kite received a direct hit right under the bomb bay before they dropped their load. First to go were the two port motors, then the inner starboard, and finally the outer starboard. With the American line only 70 kilometres to the north, Payne hoped he could glide to safety, until he realised that his fuel-lines had also been cut. As the fuselage started to be swamped by fuel spillage, making the plane highly flammable, Payne ordered his crew to bail out via the front nose hatch so he could count them as they did. But then, as Firkins writes:

> He began unstrapping himself, thinking they had all gone, when the rear-gunner presented himself, complete with parachute trailing behind. The rip cord had accidentally caught something as he was making his way up to the nose. Looking at one another in horror, Payne ordered him back to find the spare chute which was supposed to have been carried in bombers on all operations. The gunner came back and reported he could not find it; later it transpired that it had been taken out to be packed and not returned before take-off.

Payne had two options. He could leave his rear-gunner to his fate and jump and fight his own battle for survival, relying on the mandatory provisions in the escape kit.

The other option for Payne was to try to fly his enflamed bomber down and attempt a crash-landing that might give them both a chance of survival. He opted to prepare to land, and soon found himself flying into a head-wind, making straight for tension wires. He was faced with another hasty decision: to go above or below them. He chose the latter, and while the lines cut off the top of his tail fins, he still managed to land in a farm field. Miraculously, the impact of the landing extinguished the fire in the port-outer engine.

But as the two crewmen leapt from the plane, they were confronted by a group of excited ten-year-old Hitler youths wielding Tommy-guns. Thankfully, the boys were calmed down by an elder home-guard and the pair were saved to spend the last few weeks of the war as POWs.

Payne was never decorated, but Firkins adds that 'his action was symbolic of the spirit of the squadron which had built up a record and reputation second to none during its service in Bomber Command'. But Payne did have one legacy, albeit dubious: he was the second last crew from Bomber Command to be shot down in World War II.

Operation 28: The Hague, Tuesday 30 April
Spam dropping near The Hague. Had a great welcome from people. – Flying time (day): 3hrs 00mins

Operation 29: Rotterdam, Wednesday 1 May
Supply dropping near Rotterdam. – Flying time (day): 3hrs 15mins

Operation 30: Rotterdam, Friday 3 May
Supply dropping near Rotterdam. Weather still very squally. – Flying time (day): 2hrs 45mins

Flying hours for 460 Squadron
Operational: *56hrs 00mins (day), 140hrs 35mins (night)*
Non-operational: *19hrs 55mins (day), 22hrs 20mins (night)*
Total: *75hrs 55mins (day), 162hrs 55mins (night)*

YEAR		AIRCRAFT		Pilot, or 1st Pilot	2nd Pilot, Pupil or Passenger	DUTY (Including Results and Remarks)
Month	Date	Type	No.			
—	—	—	—	—	—	—— Totals Brought Forward
MAY	3	LANCASTER III	G2	SELF	F/O EMERSON	30TH. OPERATION
					SGT ENTWISTLE	SUPPLY DROPPING NEAR
					F/S MURRAY	ROTTERDAM. 4 BLOCKS
					F/S FORD	OF 284 SACKS. 416 MLS
					F/S FREEZER	WEATHER STILL VERY
					F/S FIRKINS	SQUALLY

F. Lawrence S/L
O.C. 'C' FLIGHT

[signature] W/C.
C.O. 460 SQUADRON.

SUMMARY FOR. MAY.		TYPES.
UNIT	460 SQUADRON	LANCASTER I
DATE	5.5.45	LANCASTER III
SIGNATURE	[signature]	

TOTAL HOURS FOR 460 SQUADRON.

Chapter 9

Those Australian Airmen

'We stood dancing and jumping and waving like
mad, so that our arms flew almost out of joint.'

Jannie Verstigen

ON 1 MAY 1945, JANNIE VAN SPLUNDER had cause for a special
entry in her secret wartime diary, special because at long last
they were words of joy. As Flying Officer Keith Bennett's day
began as usual at Binbrook, the day also started much as it
had for the last five years for Jannie. Her parents' home was
still swarming with Germans while she and her family were still
forced to live in her father's office. But by the time the day had
drawn to a close, she and her family could finally believe – not
only hope – that the war was coming to an end.

In the immediate term, at least she knew she would now
be able to eat. For this Jannie could thank the swarming mass
of low-flying Lancaster bombers that had dropped tonnes of
food and medical supplies over her homeland. Having seen

the Lancasters pass over the village so many times previously en route to Germany or other target zones, to know that this time the objective was a humanitarian one filled everyone involved – those who received the food, and those who dropped it – with joy.

The following is an English version of Jannie's diary from that momentous day. Like many Dutch people who benefited from the food-drops, her memories of the event still bring tears to her eyes.

In the afternoon of 1 May 1945 I had to go to typing lessons at Mr Oosthock's on the Lagendyk. We had just begun when we heard aeroplanes and saw them circle over Rotterdam. When returning they flew right over our heads. How beautiful: they were dark-coloured English aeroplanes with a circle on the bottom. They came rushing on and skimmed over – inspiring, and almost monstrously big across the fields. Some of them flew right on to us, so big, so very big, so that we screamed with fear and excitement. With thunderous noise they flew away over our heads, back to England. Sometimes it was terrifying to look at, and fortunately the Germans could not and dared not do anything about it. I think the aeroplanes flew so very low on purpose so that the Germans should feel deeply impressed.

We hung out of the window yelling and screaming, yes really screaming; we could not help doing so when again a plane came rushing on, we simply had to cry. At last we could not stand it any longer and our typing teacher and we [my fellow pupils and I] sprinted as fast as we could to the New Road [main road to Rotterdam]. On the way we jumped on the back of the bicycles of two boys [so] that we arrived at the viaduct quicker, Ineke [Bouwine's nickname] and I. On the viaduct to Rijsoord a crowd of people stood on the lookout. We saw the vastness of fields and meadows around us, the concrete road stretched out straight in front of us. The aeroplanes did not fly that low any longer. We thought it a pity, but then suddenly a large scream rang out! A number of aeroplanes came alarmingly low rushing along! In our direction! Keeping straight on! We stood dancing and jumping and waving like mad, so that our arms flew almost out of joint. One of the planes flew over so very low that we could see the pilots and some of us saw them wave a white handkerchief. And what happened? A packet came down and fell below the viaduct. One of the men got hold of it. Out of a jute bag the man pulled an oblong white box. People crowded around him in such a way that he could hardly loosen the string. Out of the box came ten packets of cigarettes! The man distributed them to different men and they shared them with others. In each parcel were two rows of ten cigarettes, so there were 200 cigarettes altogether! We also tried to get hold of one cigarette, and Ineke got one, she wanted to keep it as a souvenir forever. Most of the men and boys lit the cigarettes immediately, but others kept them. The aeroplane had disappeared meanwhile, but gave the airmen's salute as a farewell by swaying down with one wing and then upwards again with the other wing. Fantastic!

Although I did not obtain a cigarette, I also have something as a souvenir. For the airmen had enclosed a piece of paper with their names written on it in a hurry. I copied these names on the rail of the viaduct and Ineke and I shall write to them a letter after the war in order to thank them for the great help they gave our people. This I wrote down on a sheet I tore out of my memo book, an old one from 1941. It reads: Royal Australian Air Force, Alby Murray, 116 High Street, West Maitland, NSW, Australia (Van Diemens Land), and Keith Bennett, 33 Mathews Av., Lane Cove, Sydney Australia.

We think this [is] such a wonderful incident, we talk about it over and over again. It will be so nice to write them after the war, but of course the war with the Japanese has to come to an end first of all, otherwise it is impossible to send a letter to Australia. It sounds so very adventurous. How we shall thank them and beg them to answer us, if only one word on a picture postcard. There were more aeroplanes flying past, but we were paying such close attention to the parcel that we forgot to wave at them. Eventually no more aeroplanes came and we returned home, talking excitedly with each other.

Jannie's excitement was shared by many throughout western Holland as the Allies carried out their food-drops all over the region. The Germans attempted to convince the Dutch that the food-drops had been made possible due to their acquiescence but such propaganda went unheeded by a Dutch population swept up in emotion by the sight of Allied bombers dropping their loads and signalling the airman's wave, as did Flying Officer Bennett in the G2 Lancaster over Ridderkerk. They knew that their starvation would abate and that the war was just days from coming to an end – with the very real possibility that Germany would face harsh retribution.

Typical of the Germans' desperate attempt at spin on the Allied-led humanitarian operation was an alert published in the 1 May edition of the local newspaper, *Het Volk*, that the Germans had made their own during their occupation. It is re-published in *Memories of a Miracle: Operation Manna–Chowhound* by Dutch war historian Hans Onderwater.

The alert came from the Höhere SS und Polizeiführer Nordwest und Generalkommissar für das Sicherheitswesen – the German agency in occupied Holland that was feared for its brutal treatment of the Jews and anyone who dared to resist deployment to labour camps.

It read: 'As it seems to be impossible to realise food supply transports by ships, air transport has been agreed upon. Thanks to the co-operation of the German Supreme Command in the Netherlands, it has become possible that Allied aircraft drop food at designated areas, via previously determined routes without being shot at. This way the danger of scrimmages, unfair distribution and losses by foodstuffs ending up in the water has been prevented.'

The alert announced that food supplies would be distributed by the Netherlands Food Distribution Service and declared the drop-sites out of bounds to anyone not part of the collection teams. It warned: 'Violations of the prohibition will be punished with the utmost severity.'

The underground Dutch newspaper *The Flying Dutchman*, published in Dutch in London and dropped over Europe by Allied airforces, ran a warning to the Dutch people from their government in London in its 3 May 1945 edition. They were told to abide by the distribution regulations, and to withhold calls for retribution on the soon-to-be vanquished Germans. The government implored the Dutch to 'ensure a just and speedy distribution of the supplied food. Do not enter the black market with the saving of food for the starving. As difficult as it may be, do not start premature demonstrations. The arrival of the Allied lorries does not mean that you have been liberated. The government asks for self-control.'

The recollections of one sixteen-year-old boy from Rotterdam of the first Operation Manna drop on 29 April 1945 (published in *Memories of a Miracle*) expresses the gratitude of the Dutch. The boy's father had been sent to the German work camps in November 1944 but there was still no word from him, even if he was alive or dead. His mother had struggled, as thousands had, to find food. In desperation, she sold her father's gold watch and a golden chain to buy potatoes and beans.

But as the boy would recall as a 64-year-old, on 29 April 1945 fate did finally shine on him and the Dutch:

I will never in my life forget that day. The day before we had heard on the radio that the British would drop food. This rumour had been going around for some time but the Jerries had said this was impossible and that they would shoot all these English out of the sky. Mother said that she believed in miracles but not in nonsense. That day I walked from Dorpsweg in Rotterdam-South to the Kleidijk in Rhoon where we had a friend living who was willing to give us some wheat. Around noon I slowly walked around the Kleidijk and suddenly it looked as if I saw little dots in the skies. Aircraft were the last things I thought of. If an aeroplane flew that low it was either a German or a Tommie in distress. After a few minutes I witnessed the greatest miracle in my life. They were big black English bombers, over a hundred. They came closer and closer and made a tremendous noise. You could see the men inside. They flew to Waalhaven, no longer used by the Germans. It had been blocked with poles, and ditches had been dug to make it unsuitable for aircraft to land. The British bombers flew low over the field and then suddenly all sorts of things fell out. I stood on the dyke and once a few had passed I started scream-ing, dancing and waving. It is silly, but at a moment like that you think that these men can see and hear you. Whether it is true or not, I still believe that they did hear

149

me. For a while I stood there one aircraft came very close. I think it flew about 50 metres high. I looked at the cockpit and I saw this man looking at me. Then he slowly raised his hand and waved at me. I stood there while the tears were running down my cheeks and thought: 'Mamma, this is your miracle.' Then I looked around me and saw that the Kleidijk was full of people who cheered and waved like I did.

In the same book, Yyvonne Boichel from Wassenaar recounts the food-drops, in particular one box that landed in her family garden when they were standing in it. The episode, marked by the sound of a huge crash, highlighted the inherent danger of wayward disposal by the Lancasters: that of such bags landing on and maiming – if not killing – civilians. Thankfully, none in her family was hurt; but she remembers the message on the bags being in Dutch and German with contrasting tones of sympathy.

The message in Dutch read: 'These foodstuffs are for you. They are brought to you by Allied airmen and are meant for Dutch civilians only. Search the entire area in case a parcel has fallen outside the designated areas and add it to your supplies. Do not use the foodstuffs until your leaders in charge have divided them and you have received your rightful portion. If the enemy tries to steal it write down all relevant information and report this. Keep on looking for us. We will come back.'

But as Boichel points out, the German translation of the message was 'much less friendly'. 'It told the Germans that food was for us and not them' and it also warned that any German who dared to take any parcel would be treated as a war criminal and would be punished as such. 'They were also told to help us as much as they could,' she says. 'But we had a problem. We were so very hungry. We would have loved to open the parcel and eat from it. But father said we had to hand it in. Then I carefully cut the message from the top of the box. I had it framed and it still hangs on my wall.'

But as an extract from a letter published in *Memories of a Miracle* reveals, the occupying German forces also faced a dilemma when, inevitably, some boxes landed near their camp bases in western Holland. One German paratrooper who is named in the book as 'Horst N. from Velbert, Germany' said on one occasion the boxes were dropped by a USAF bomber.

It may have meant food for the Dutch, but for me it meant that Germany was finished. Funnily enough, a lot fell near our camp. Our commander ordered us to carry everything to the Dutch. A soldier who kept only a few tins with cigarettes was punished. Bloody ridiculous, for after the British landings at Arnhem we had been smoking their cigarettes for weeks. Four days later I was a POW. The first things they gave me when the Canadians arrived were cigarettes. They found out that I was a paratrooper and not an SS man. I was put in charge of cutting portions into smaller ones for distribution. It was the first time in weeks that I had a decent meal.

The impact of Operations Manna and Chowhound was huge, presenting massive logistical challenges for the Dutch. In the words of Dutch Royal Prince Bernard: 'My entire staff and I lived under the greatest tension during the last weeks before the surrender. The tension was greater than even during the invasion, because during these last weeks each Dutchman wanted to save as many Dutchmen as possible from certain death by starvation. For us this was the most important period of the entire war.'

So important was the combined humanitarian effort that it became the subject of a play shown at the stadium in Rotterdam less than two years after the war ended. The audience of 60,000 people included Queen Wilhelmina, Prince Bernard and the two Princesses. Jannie Van Splunder was among the audience, and she described the experience in a letter to Keith Bennett: 'As soon as they entered, everyone began to sing "Wilhelmina". It was unforgettable.'

The play, starring hundreds of actors, covered the pre-war years, the occupation, the famine, liberation, and what was then the immediate postwar era. But, as Jannie told Bennett, the simulated arrival of planes dropping food parcels as they did in Operations Manna and Chowhound was a pivotal moment: 'Suddenly aeroplanes came over, a lot of them, and dropped large sheets of paper which [were] meant to represent the food parcels. The whole stadium filled with [the] clapping and hurrahs of the people, and we waved enthusiastically at the planes. It was just as if it was May 1945 again!' Even as the Van Splunders were heading back to their home in Ridderkerk, they could not help but remark that 'it had been as if we had experienced everything again'.

The gratitude of the Dutch is no better expressed than in one of the thousands of cards and letters of thanks that were sent to airmen like Bennett and their squadron after the war. One such letter sent to the RAF included the 'Ballad of the Allied Bombers that brought Food to Hungered Holland.' It reads:

Then said the Lord: Behold I will rain bread
from Heaven for you – but how could we believe it?
Our best men have gone, away in prison or dead,
a famished people left behind to grieve it.
If God's bread came, would we like to receive it?
But He said: In the morning, lo, before your eyes
there comes His Manna dropping from the skies.

For thundering along the vault of heaven
wave upon wave of planes came roaring over.
No shot is fired, no siren warning given:
a peaceful raid before the war is over.
We keep our breaths. The very birds that hover
and hang about the sky stricken with awe expect
their giant brethren's deeds, who swerve about, direct
their course to mellow fields speckled with flowers
    and clover
where lapwings play and singing larks arise,
and there drop tonnes of manna from the skies!

It's terrible to pray for bombs to fall,
knowing you may be killed, yet to continue
to pray because you know that after all
nothing but bombs can cut the enemy's sinew;
to fear and yet to pray with all that's in you:
God, let them fall, for we must win this war!
Rather be killed than crushed and trampled o'er
by those who hate because they cannot win you.
Our prayer was heard and bombs of every size
rained down, a devilish manna, from the skies.

All this is over now. We look on high,
and planes that carried death and devastation
to foe and friend alike now fill the sky,
drop boons instead of bombs and bring salvation
to friendly people of a friendly nation –
They prove the promise ringing in our ear
that all men shall be free from want and fear,
they are the Charter's tactual revelation –
no fear or want where'er the bomber flies
that drops its tonnes of manna from the skies.

Pilots who come to us even while waging
the bloodiest war that ever yet befell
mankind and that for five years has been raging
around and o'er us, making life a hell –
look how we wave at you! Now all is well.

Look how we raise our children on our shoulder.
We promise they'll be men and women bolder
and better than we are, and that they'll tell
their children's children when they're old and wise
how men like Gods dropped manna from the skies.

Year		Aircraft		Pilot, or 1st Pilot	2nd Pilot, Pupil or Passenger	Duty (Including Results and Remarks)
Month	Date	Type	No.			
—		—		—	—	—— Totals Brought Forward
May	3	Lancaster III	G₂	Self	F/O Emerson	30th. Operation
					Sgt Entwistle	Supply dropping near
					F/S Murray	Rotterdam. 4 Blocks
					T/S Ford	of 284 sacks. 416 mls
					T/S Freezer	Weather still very
					F/S Firkins	squally

7. Lawrence S/L
O.C. 'C' Flight

J. Hewson W/c.
C.O. 460 Squadron.

SUMMARY FOR. May   Types.
Unit   460 Squadron   Lancaster I
Date   5·5·45   Lancaster III
Signature R.W.R......

TOTAL HOURS FOR 460 SQUADRON.

Chapter 10

A Day Like No Other

On the job of supplying again. Had a wizard time
shooting up all the villages not flooded from
Rotterdam to the coast – including the Jerrys.
Dropped a carton of cigarettes with my name and
Alby's name. Saw mob of kids grab it.
A good show on tonight – One Night in Rio.

Keith Bennett, 1 May 1945

IT WAS A DAY THAT BEGAN LIKE MOST – early, with the call to 'ops'
and the pre-flight briefing by the squadron Commanding Officer,
followed by the traditional meal of eggs and bacon before take-
off. Keith Bennett's crew was one of nineteen from 460 Squadron
picked to take part in an operation that would – on this occasion
– include 227 bombers from 33 squadrons. In its entirety of ten
days it would involve an estimated 5500 sorties by 3158 RAF
aircraft, as well as another 2189 USAF planes who were carrying
out their own similarly motivated operation.

For Bennett and his crew, there was one major difference between this sortie (and the one previous) and the 26 earlier flights they had made for their highly decorated Australian squadron: instead of bombs, the plane would be loaded with desperately needed food supplies for nearly half a million starving Dutch victims of the war. And the target, at long last, would not be Germany, but Rotterdam.

The nature of their mission buoyed the crew as they waited for their G2 to be loaded with four blocks of 240 bags of supplies. 'We prepared for our trip feeling very elated and happy,' wrote Bennett in his first letter to Jannie Van Splunder in the Netherlands, dated 22 March 1946. 'The ground staff loaded on the food in the bomb compartments. After testing our engines, we set off from our aerodrome near Grimsby.'

The crew was still buzzing from the previous day when they took part in a similar sortie that was the second official drop of Operation Manna, as Bennett's diary of Tuesday 30 April reads: 'Actually flew today on a most interesting op. We dropped four blocks of 230 bags on a drome near The Hague. The Jerries kept the truce arranged for this. We flew over The Hague low. The whole population must have turned out to cheer us – many people waved sheets and flags. It was a real pleasure to do such an appreciated job.'

In all – as per its thousands of bombing raids – 460 Squadron contributed one of the most significant number of drops during Operation Manna. Lasting a period of ten days, the operation totalled one tenth – or 1000 tonnes – of the total tonnage of food dropped that saved an overall estimate of one and a half million lives, and about 1000 Dutch people per day.

Operation Manna was the result of careful planning and whatever diplomacy could be mustered when the extent of the Nazi atrocities was becoming more and more apparent.

The call to save western Holland from starvation came in January 1945 from Queen Wilhelmina to the United States president, Franklin Roosevelt, and King George VI of Great Britain. The Queen, Prince Bernard and the Dutch government had learned of their people's plight via the Resistance who sent their agents to London to inform them of the tragedy.

During the early months of 1945, rumours of a food-drop had been circulating. But it was on 17 April of that year that those rumours started becoming a real plan. The man put in charge of co-ordinating the mission was Air Commodore Andrew James Wray Geddes who was given his orders by General Walter Bedell-Smith, the chief-of-staff of General Dwight Eisenhower. Geddes, who was then the Air Commodore of Operations and Plans at the Second Tactical Air Force headquarters in Brussels, had become used to hearing about various objectives and weighing up their comparative risks based on, among other things, estimates about which side would sustain more deaths. But for Geddes, Operation Manna became an exception because the objective was purely about saving lives – and many.

In *Memories of a Miracle*, Geddes recalls his shock after being told his brief by General Bedell-Smith in Reims:

What he said caught me by complete surprise: 'Geddes, the Dutch are starving, their food is running out, the Germans cannot feed them anymore. We are being pushed by the whole Dutch government, by the President, by Churchill. Something has to be done to put an end to this tragedy. I want to see you again with a plan to feed 3,500,000 Dutch by air, drop-zones, corridors, the lot. You have my full support. Bert Harris has been told to give you two bomb groups and sufficient Pathfinders, the 8th Air Force has three Wings at your disposal. We need a prepared agreement for Jerry, no negotiations just instructions. Do it, Geddes, do it quickly. If you need any help, come to me. I will make sure Ike backs you all the way. We have cleared an office for you here. Tell me what you need and who and I will get it for you. Thank you.' That was all.

Geddes promptly went about trying to put the plan together – studying intelligence reports, maps of Holland, and then orchestrating how such an operation should be carried out. There was also the question of how the bomber crews might react when informed of the mission, and told that they could trust the Germans not to shoot back at them. It was a dramatic way for Geddes to experience the final days of the war, as it was for everyone involved.

Geddes prepared to move to the small Dutch town of Achterveld where a conference would be held between all parties to settle on terms of the operation. Simultaneously, up on the higher echelons of politics under which Geddes sat, it was not until 23 April 1945 that General Eisenhower was given the green light by the US, Great Britain and Russia to open official talks with the Reichskommissar, Dr Arthur Seyss-Inquart, about allowing an Allied-led air-drop of food and supplies which the Austrian had indicated earlier he would consider.

In the meantime, anticipating that the plan would go ahead, Allied planes and crews had been executing practice runs in England with simulated drops to gauge what size loads could be dropped at what heights and from what distance without them exploding upon impact or getting lost. And as is made clear by the comments of Kenneth E. Davey of RAF 186 Squadron, there was plenty of trial and error to get it right.

We carried out tests with 55 lb bags dropped from 1000 feet. The sacks burst, the potatoes arrived smashed, the flour bags exploded like smoke bombs and the tougher items were distributed all over the landscape. Subsequent tests at 900, 800, then 600 feet made little difference. At 500 feet, however, which for a Lancaster was skimming the treetops, the potatoes landed un-smashed and if we put them in two sacks, one inside the other, only the interior sack burst. The problem was partly solved by the armourers who adapted incendiary bomb containers which could carry 1250 lbs of supplies in the bomb bays but much more could be carried if sacks were also loaded into the fuselage to be heaved out of the door by the crew members.

The 'solution', however, was much easier in theory as the sacks they needed at such brief notice were in short supply. But soon enough, a nearby US Air Force base came forward to say that they could provide the sacks.

An approach was duly made and the US colonel was sympathetic and admitted to having vast quantities of sacks which he would be delighted to hand over – as soon as he had authority. Such an unusual request would probably have to go to the Pentagon in an infinite series of small steps before being agreed to and the chances of getting it in 24 hours – zero. There was a silence, then: 'Of course,' the Colonel added, 'petty theft is a big problem and there aren't enough MPs to guard every-thing. Especially when the hangar isn't locked and the MPs are all on the other side of the base as they will be this evening. I don't suppose anything would be noticed until at least twenty minutes after the last sack left.' A nod is as good as a wink, hands were shaken and there followed a very busy evening: 1500 heavy sand-bags went unexpectedly missing that night. The local police were around at our base the next morning. The Chief Inspector went through the motions [saying]: 'Americans seem to have lost a few bags. Don't suppose you chaps know anything about it? No? Well, I'll just note that for the record.' He closed his notebook and was taken off for a gin and tonic in the officers' mess. Over a drink it was soon clear that the affair held little mystery for him but he was a man who knew real priorities when he saw them.

The original plan for the operation was that the Stirlings and Halifaxes from Transport Command's No. 38 Group would execute the operation, but the loads that would be dropped were too large for these planes to accommodate. Hence, the operation was handed to Bomber Command. Pencilled in to carry it out were 33 squadrons made up of Lancasters from No. 1 and 3 Groups, as well as Lancasters and Mosquitoes from No. 8 Group, also known as the Pathfinder Force.

The first drop – a trial-run by two Lancasters agreed to between the Red Cross and the Germans – was set for 27 April, a day before parties representing the two warring sides were due to have their first face-to-face meeting at Achterveld to settle on the official truce and its terms. But the drop was postponed to 28 April due to poor weather. And while conditions that day again forced the drop to be held over for yet another day, the scheduled talks between the Allies and Germans across the Canadian lines in Achterveld went ahead. Eisenhower and Seyss-Inquart were not in attendance – their first talks would be held two days later, on 30 April, the same day Adolf Hitler committed suicide in his Berlin bunker.

At the negotiating table in this first meeting at Achterveld was a delegation of Germans including a Dr Ernst Schwebel, Dr Plutzar, Major Stoeckle and Lieutenant Von Mossow who would cross paths with Geddes again. Representing the Allies with Geddes were Field Marshall Montgomery's chief-of-staff,

Sir Francis de Guingand, who was also a friend of Geddes and known to him as 'Freddie'. The meeting was held in the village school which Canadian forces had surrounded with a barbed-wire fence. The image of the Germans arriving in Canadian staff cars remains very clear to Geddes: 'When they arrived I stood under the trees where the cars stopped. They all carried white flags. The Germans were escorted into the building and told to wait to be presented to Freddie [de Guingand]. I had the chance to have a good look at them. There were four chaps. One looked like a Party boss, the others were officers. They showed their credentials to Freddie who handed them to me. Not a word was spoken.'

Geddes also recalls their idiosyncrasies: Major Stoeckle was the only one who made the Nazi salute; Dr Plutzar, who spoke English, protested that the Canadian soldiers should call him 'Fritz'; Dr Schwebel had a big nose and facial scars from duelling at university; and Lieutenant Von Mossow, a para-trooper, was noted for his silence which led the Allies to suspect him of gathering intelligence information.

The talks did not conclude with a firm agreement. De Guingand told the Germans of Geddes' plan, stressed that speed was essential, and suggested in no uncertain terms that both sides get cracking so that Dutch lives could be saved. Schwebel's response was disconcerting. He said he had not come to settle on a deal, but to hear what the Allies had to propose, and to report back to Reichskommissar Seyss-Inquart on the outcome of the meeting. This was not what de Guingand wanted to hear, and he became angry. The stalemate further intensified when Schwebel said he would want to talk to General Eisenhower face to face before signing off on any agreement, believing that his status entitled him to meet with the highest-ranked Allied general rather than his second-in-command, as de Guingand was.

Even as the Germans continued to deliberate over a settlement on the agreement, the Allies – frustrated, and knowing that up to 1000 Dutch people were dying every day – boldly decided to order a test-run just to see how the Germans would react. In the absence of a clear agreement, the danger of the exercise was clear to all. There was no guarantee that the unarmed Lancasters, travelling under 500 feet and fully exposed in daylight, would not be shot down by the enemy. Nobody knew how the Germans would react when confronted by the sight of the planes swooping en masse into German-occupied Holland. Indeed, even after the truce was in force, there were still lingering suspicions on both sides that one would shoot the other; or in the case of the Allies, that the Germans would fail to fire off a red warning flare to any Allied plane that accidentally flew outside the agreed flight corridor into a danger zone, as per the conditions.

As Bob Upcott, the first pilot of the first of two Lancaster bombers to fly into Holland for the trial-drop, remembers:

> We had to fly low to the targets to be able to drop the food without damaging it. We were told to carry no ammunition for our guns and we had to stay within a strictly confined corridor while over Holland for our

approach and away from the target area. We were not only excited about the food-drops, we were also scared. We had been flying over Holland at altitude of 15,000 to 20,000 feet on our way to targets in Germany and all of a sudden we are asked to fly at 400 feet, while the German soldiers were still manning the 88 mm and 105 mm flak guns near the corridor we had to fly through. Our two bombers had to fly through a corridor that the Germans had prescribed. If our mission was a success and we could drop our food without being shot at, Operation Manna would be launched.

On 29 April, 246 Lancasters and eighteen Mosquitoes loaded with 535 tonnes of food and supplies took off into the rain. Upcott remembers that first flight: 'Crossing the Channel we flew on instruments because it was still misty. Over the continent the weather cleared and we could see.'

But what Upcott and his crew saw as they approached the target zone of Duindigt racecourse just outside Utrecht was rather disconcerting: German anti-aircraft guns were aimed at the Lancasters, German flags still flew over the German-occupied buildings and German troops were still stationed at their vantage points on railroad bridges and canals. 'We were looking right down a number of barrels,' Upcott recalls. 'We were very lucky that they observed the truce and held their fire.' Well, not all of them *did* hold their fire. Upon return to England it became clear that a number of planes had been hit by hand-gun fire – as would often happen throughout the duration of

Operation Manna. As Upcott stresses, the fear that the German flak and tank guns would open on the Lancasters was very real, especially in the absence of a truce. As he says:

> No agreement had been signed when the first Lancasters approached occupied Holland. At an extremely low altitude of 100 to 1000 feet, the large four-engine bombers would have been an easy prey for the many anti-aircraft guns. Even if the Germans had opened fire and killed hundreds of young Britons and other Allies, they would have had the right to do so. The responsible commanders of the RAF knew the risk they took, knew the terrible tragedy that could have happened over Holland if the Germans had opened fire. Above all, they knew that any German reaction would be legitimate. The commanders knew it, so did the pilots and their crew members.

Despite Upcott's drop overshooting the mark, the trial-run was deemed a success. And by noon that same day, BBC Radio informed its listeners in England and Holland that Operation Manna would start that very same day. 'To think that today we did good instead of blowing towns and people to hell makes me realise that there is still some good left in this world,' Upcott remarks.

~

Meanwhile, the deliberations and negotiations between the Allies and the Germans continued. Two days after the first official rendezvous between the Allies and occupiers – and one day after the first trial-drop on 29 April – the long-awaited meeting with Seyss-Inquart to finalise all the fine-point details was held at Achterveld. Seyss-Inquart arrived with a number of German army, navy and airforce officers as well as Dutch civil servants to provide the Allies with precise on-the-ground explanations of the food crisis and the state of the surviving Dutch people.

The meeting was not without its twists, in particular, a mischievous plan to unsettle Seyss-Inquart. Among those who came to Achterveld as part of the Allied contingent was Prince Bernard, the commander-in-chief of the Dutch forces under Allied command, and of the Resistance that operated in the occupied territory of western Holland. Particularly galling to the Reichskommissar was that the Prince arrived at the meeting in the black Mercedes staff car that was previously Seyss-Inquart's – until the Dutch Resistance confiscated it, gave it a new number plate and handed it to the beloved Royal as a present. Then they parked the car exactly where Seyss-Inquart was due to arrive in the Canadian staff car.

Though humiliating Seyss-Inquart was not the objective of the day – the goal being to organise the mammoth task of Operation Manna – the Allies could not resist the chance to remind the Austrian who held the upper hand. And according to Geddes, it was an effective ploy. 'I did not see the incident, but later I spoke to Colonel Van Houten, Prince Bernard's chief-of-staff, who told me that Seyss-Inquart was very upset indeed. It was quite a humiliation to get out of a Canadian Packard to

see your own car standing there with big white stars on the
hood and the bonnet, a shield saying CNF-1 and a young Allied
general leaning on it, clearly showing off that he is the new
proprietor.'

The rest of the day was spent churning through a relentless
schedule of meetings and work-groups. Also in attendance for
the Allies were de Guingand, Geddes' senior officer, General
Bedell-Smith; General Calloway from the Canadian forces, who
would take command of the soon-to-be-liberated region of
western Holland; and General Ivan Suslaparov from the
Russian forces, whose aim was to ensure no Allied agreement
was made without the knowledge of his commanding officers.
There were also numerous sailors and army representatives
whose purpose was to organise the practical side of getting food
back into western Holland by sea and land following the air-
drops, and to ensure that a system of collection and distribution
was in place.

The mood throughout the day was far from congenial. In his
meetings, Seyss-Inquart was bluntly warned that any breach of
terms would be severely dealt with. And as Geddes recalls, the
Germans were reminded of their culpability for the crisis. 'At
about twelve o' clock we took a break. The Germans were put
under guard in a classroom where we served them a straight-
forward meal of combat rations. The Dutch were invited to join
us for lunch. We entertained them, gave them the best food we
had, and almost embarrassed them with cigarettes, sweets and
other goodies.'

At the end of a meeting that followed lunch, General

Reichalet, chief-of-staff to the German commander in charge, finally put pen to paper on all matters relating to the agreement for Operation Manna. It was six o' clock in the evening. With the ink barely dry, he promptly left.

The following day, 1 May – as the initial Operation Manna food-drops continued successfully – Geddes took the signed documents to a rendezvous point in no-man's-land west of Wageningen for a meeting with the Germans. Travelling under Canadian escort, he presented maps and documents pertaining to Operation Manna. Among the Germans was Lieutenant Von Massow, the stony-faced paratrooper Geddes had encountered at that first meeting at Achterveld. Armed with German intelligence, Geddes could not resist the opportunity to rattle Von Massow. As he says, 'I decided to play my trick against the cocky behaviour of Von Massow.'

While the group smoked cigarettes, he took Von Massow aside to inform him of how strong the allied Advances really were by showing him the latest issue of *Stars and Stripes* – then a weekly US forces newspaper, which still exists in print and internet form today, but which was founded in 1861 during the Civil War for Union troops. The newspaper was resurrected during World War I and then closed again, before returning once more in World War II, from 18 April 1942, when it was printed in London.

Von Massow's response to seeing the newspaper was typical: 'Propaganda,' Geddes reports him saying. Geddes continues: '"That may be true," I said. "But I want you to know that your brother General Kurt Von Massow is OK and well. We bagged him near Kassel a few days ago." Von Massow's mouth fell wide open. He turned around, said something to the others, jumped into his jeep and roared off. On our way back [group captain and driver] Hill asked what the matter was with the German lieutenant. "Nothing," I said. "I gave him his brother's best wishes."'

Geddes' role in Operation Manna had come to an end, and two days later he was back in Brussels at the Second Tactical Air Force headquarters.

~

The load for each Lancaster in Operation Manna weighed approximately two tonnes, and was generally made up of flour, dehydrated meat and luncheon meat, margarine, vegetables, dried egg powder, soup, tea, yeast powder, chocolate, and emergency medical supplies. Loading up the Lancasters with supplies rather than bombs was a lot harder for the ground crew. Because of the load's bulk, it took up to 16 hours for a ground crew to pack a Lancaster for one food-drop that would take about three to four hours to implement. The bomb bays were jammed with sacks and boxes that were positioned on sheets of metal hammered in the rough shape of the bomb doors and propped with lengths of wood. In time, the bomb bay doors became disfigured from the stress of holding such heavy loads.

Supplies for the first mission totalled about 500 tonnes. Food was dropped over six different designated zones near the towns of Valkenburg, the Duindigt racecourse, Ypenburg and Waalhaven, with about 90 percent of them hitting their target.

171

Those among the Dutch who were not ravaged by malnutrition and disease volunteered to help collect, store and hand out the goods under the watchful eye of the Dutch police who set up distribution centres throughout western Holland. This was not only to prevent looting – which did occur – nor just to prevent people walking into drop-zones and getting hit – which also happened. It also served to ensure that rations were distributed fairly and safely. One of the biggest risks for victims of starvation is exposing the body to too much food too quickly. After an extended period without nourishment, the body needs to slowly accustom itself to renewed supply.

In the course of the nine days that followed 29 April, some 7030 tonnes of supplies were dropped in about 5500 sorties by Lancasters representing 33 squadrons from Nos. 1, 3 and 8 groups, the latter being the Pathfinders force. On 1 May, the Americans emulated the mission in an exercise called Operation Chowhound. The United States Air Force committed B-17 Flying Fortresses from 37 squadrons and ultimately dropped 3710 tonnes of supplies in 5334 sorties.

Despite giving the ultimate sign-off for Operation Manna, the Germans remained suspicious throughout the duration of the mission. Instead of dropping food, they feared the Allies would offload more paratroopers. Hence, they placed anti-aircraft guns at each designated drop-zone and checked the contents of the packages, making sure that they contained food and supplies rather than human cargo.

Bennett and his crew were well aware of the Germans' jumpiness – and hence the impending danger – as they prepared for their Rotterdam drop on May 1. Before taking off from Binbrook in overcast weather, Bennett gave a small package to rear-gunner Peter Firkins. It contained a bundle that he and bomb-aimer Alby Murray had hastily assembled. Attached to it was a slip of paper on which both airmen had written their names and addresses under a message in Dutch that read: *Naar U*, 'To you'. The package – contained in a small jute bag which was attached to an old hat that would be its parachute – was not destined for Rotterdam, as were the tonnes of food supplies. It was destined for a yet-to-be-determined landmark: a country town, a gathering of people, or a person to whom Keith and Alby could dedicate their mission.

After a clean take-off in rainy conditions from Binbrook, the G2 headed east and joined its fellow bombers before heading across the Channel in formation, travelling only a few hundred feet above the seas. The weather cleared once they reached Holland, then they slipped into their designated flight corridor, flying so low they could see the happiness and relief on the faces of the starving Dutch, but also the expressions of anxiety, suspicion and fear amongst the German troops who stood ready in case the Lancasters dropped bombs or released gunfire from their turrets. And the suspicion was mutual. Alby Murray has not forgotten the look of one German trooper peering up at them with his rifle aimed. Until Murray – nestled in the front-gunner's turret – gave the German the fright of his life by suddenly turning his two empty 0.303 Browning guns towards him. As Murray recalls: 'He was a big fella and just threw his arms up in the air, letting his rifle drop to the ground.'

As they continued on their journey to Rotterdam, Bennett and his crew were stunned by the devastation beneath them: the flooded fields and towns, the absence of crops and livestock, and the desperate sight of thousands of starving Dutch rushing out from their houses. As Bennett recalls in a letter to Jannie after the war: 'It shocked us to see the terrible damage done by the Germans to your countryside. Everywhere the country was flooded and farms destroyed.' And his sense of horror at what he had seen never diminished. In another letter to Jannie which he drafted on 3 December 1990 after she had sent him a documentary called *The Hunger Winter*, Bennett wrote: 'What they had to do to survive and the many who did not. I was shocked to learn how bad was the starvation and the suffering with no fuel for heating. I know it was a surprise to my surviving crew members who requested copies of the video.'

Murray admits that the Allies didn't realise the extent of the Dutch people's suffering in the aftermath of that horrible winter until they saw it up close. As he recalls: 'It's terrible to see people starving. It seemed that a lot of people didn't know about that at that particular point.' Cyril Entwistle, Bennett's flight engineer, concurs: 'We, in this country, didn't know anything about it until we were told on the squadron about these food-drops. We were absolutely ignorant about what was going on a few miles away.'

As the G2 flew over Rotterdam, they saw streams of Dutch people running and waving. 'It was marvellous, yes marvellous,' says Entwistle, 'waving hankies and all sorts of things. Of course they must have known like we did at the time that the

During the German occupation Jannie
Van Splunder (pictured) kept a daily diary which
she buried in her backyard. This is from her
1 May 1945 entry, the day Keith Bennett's crew
dropped a package of cigarettes over Ridderkerk.
She wrote down and attached the addresses
of Bennett and Alby Murray.

DE VLIEGENDE HOLLANDER

VERSPREID DOOR DE GEALLIEERDE LUCHTMACHT   LAATSTE NUMMER, 10 MEI

DUITSCHLAND CAPITULEER

In den nacht van Zondag 6 op Maandag 7 Mei 1945 onderteekenden generaal Jodl en admiraal Von Friedeburg op het Geallieerde Hoofdkwartier te Rheims de overeenkomst waarbij alle Duitsche strijdkrachten zich onvoorwaardelijk overgaven. Midden tegenover de Duitsche gedelegeerden zit de chef van Eisenhowers staf, generaal Bedell Smith. Vierde van rechts is de Russische vertegenwoordiger, generaal Soeslaparow.

Het Derde Rijk onderteekent de onvoorwaardelijke overgave
— eerst te Rheims, dan te Berlijn

In een eenvoudig klasselokaal van een Fransche ambachtsschool in de buurt van Rheims heeft Duitschland zich onvoorwaardelijk overgegeven. Tegen een achtergrond van het verlichte stafkaarten zaten vijftien mannen rond een oude gesleten tafel, die de sporen droeg van honderden scholieren, die er met hun messen in hadden zitten kerven. Voor de fotografen en filmoperateurs was een speciale verlichting geïnstalleerd, die de gezichten der deelnemenden scherp afteekende. Aan den muur een kalender met den datum: 7 Mei 1945.

Keitel, chef van het *Oberkommando der Wehrmacht* gedurende dezen Wereldoorlog, onderteekent te Berlijn Duitschlands onvoorwaardelijke overgave

Van de eene zijde der tafel zitten de drie Duitschers, Admiraal von Friedeburg, Generaal Jodl en zijn adjudant. Tegenover hen zitten Gen. Bedell-Smith, Chef van den Staf van Generaal Eisenhower, de Fransche Generaal Sevez, de Russische Generaal Soeslaparow en nog enkele andere hooge officieren en tolken. Zestien vertegenwoordigers van pers en radio zijn aanwezig.

Half drie 's morgens komt de Geallieerde delegatie binnen, Generaal Smith, de vertegenwoordiger van Gen. Eisenhower, het laatst. De sterke verlichting maakt de warm in de volle kamer. Om precies 2 uur 39 komen de Duitsche gedelegeerden binnen en blijven stram achter hun stoelen staan tot Generaal Smith hen een teeken geeft, dat zij kunnen gaan zitten. Zij zijn in uniform en zien er uitgeput uit. Generaal Smith vraagt hun of zij de beteekenis van het te onderteekenen document ten volle begrijpen. Nadat de vraag vertaald is, antwoorden zij bevestigend.

Er wordt verder geen woord gesproken en zonder een minuut te verliezen worden de papieren in veelvoud onderteekend. Om 2 uur 40 heeft Duitschland gecapituleerd.

IN DE RUÏNES VAN BERLIJN

Op 8 Mei arriveerden in Berlijn hooge Geallieerde vertegenwoordigers, teneinde in de hoofdstad van het voormalige Derde Rijk Duitschlands capitulatie te bezegelen. Met eenige moeite werd een gebouw gevonden dat niet geheel of grootendeels verwoest was: de Technische School in Karlsdorf. Russen, Engelschen en Amerikanen voerden er besprekingen tot over alle punten overeenstemming was bereikt. Toen, kort na 12 uur, mochten de Duitschers binnenkomen. Voor het Duitsche leger zou veldmaarschalk Keitel teekenen, voor de marine admiraal von Friedeburg, voor de luchtmacht generaal Stumpff.

Voor de onderteekening kwam Keitel binnen in vol ornaat, met zijn maarschalkstaf in de hand. Luchtmaarschalk Tedder, die aan Geallieerde zijde onderteekenen zou, tezamen met maarschalk Zjoekow, generaal Spaatz van de Amerikaansche Luchtmacht en generaal Delattre de Tassigny als getuigen, stelde Keitel de vraag: "Hebt U dit document van uw voorwaardelijke overgave ontvangen?" "Jawohl," Hij vroeg toen nog of de in werking stelling 24 uur kon worden uitgesteld.

Het antwoord was: "Sie können gehen!"

De overwinnaar! — Generaal Eisenhower heeft zich in dezen ... heeft zich vooral groote verdie... ... strateeg gebleken van groot for... worven door de wijze waarop hij ... van brillante generaals dat w... werkte, bijeen wist te houd... inspireeren

Germany surrenders: the page one story 'The Flying Dutchman' (*De Vliegende Hollander*) had been looking for.

Good news was the best news for the tabloid and broadsheet English press on 8 May 1945.

In Holland, euphoria, relief and tears as liberation finally came.

Back home: Keith Bennett (left) with his mother, Catherine, and father, William, on the day Bennett snr, a squadron leader with the Air Training Corps, presented him with his Distinguished Flying Cross (DFC) medal.

Keith Bennett (bottom left) after receiving his DFC, with his father, William (top centre); and his brothers, Alan, a cadet (top left); Frank, still in the Air Training Corps (top right) and Jack, who flew Kittyhawks with 77 Squadron (bottom right).

AWARDED D.F.C.

SON OF FLYING FAMILY

Mr. and Mrs. W G. Bennett, of 33 Matthews Avenue, Lane Cove, have received a cable from the Air Ministry, advising that their eldest son, Flying Officer Keith W. Bennett, R.A.A.F., has been awarded the Distinguished Flying Cross.

Keith has completed a tour of 30 operational bombing missions over Germany, including the sinking of the 'Admiral Scheer,' and the bombing of Berchtesgaden.

He was a member of the famous 460 Squadron, R.A.A.F. Of the 60,000 tons of bombs dropped by the 12 R.A.A.F Squadrons, 460's share was 29,000 tons.

Keith, who is now on his way home aboard the Aquitania, was Pilot and Skipper of 'G2', which replaced the famous G for George which is now in Australia having completed 90 missions.

Mr. and Mrs. Bennett's second son, Jack R. Bennett, is a fighter Pilot in the R.A.A.F., and has been in Labuan, Borneo, since the 9th Div. went in. He is also expected home very soon, and the Bennetts are preparing to celebrate the home coming of both of their sons.

Frank, the third son, is a Corporal in the A.T.C., and Dad, who was a Pilot in the 1914-1918 war, is a Squadron

The award of a Distinguished Flying Cross (pictured) to Keith Bennett made the news back home in Australia before he returned.

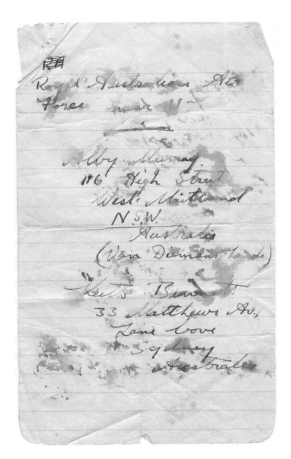

The original note Keith Bennett and Alby Murray attached to the package of cigarettes that they dropped over Ridderkerk on 1 May 1945. Note their use of the Dutch words *Naar U* ('to you') and *Van Diemen's Land*.

Flying Officer Keith Bennett DFC.

Ridderkerk, 22ⁿᵈ February 1946.

Dear Australian airman,

Probably your face will express great astonishment when you get this letter from somebody, who is quite unknown to you. So first I'll tell you who I am. I am a Dutch girl, nineteen years old, and I live at Ridderkerk. I want to write to you, because I will tell you how grateful we are to you and your fellow-flyers for all you have done for us!

Last year your aeroplanes dropped innumerable boxes full of delicious food on Holland and you saved us from starving! In those days we were almost crazy with joy and excitement and all people waved and screamed at the huge machines which often flew so low, that we could see the pilot. The cruel Germans looked very angrily at the running and crying people, but this time they dared not say a word, which was very seldom the case, however! One day, again a group of aeroplanes came rushing over the polders of our village and one of them (your machine!) dropped a packet! It fell down near the viaduct over the mainroad from Rotterdam to Dordrecht. Some people told that they had seen a flying-man wave a white handkerchief. Were that you? We gazed in amazement after the big aeroplane and then we saw that it greeted us, for it heeled over from one side to the other! In our language this is called "de vliegrgroet": "the airman's greeting". And then we ran and pushed and cried, till at last a man could get hold of the parcel. He unpacked it a white box and it contained a sheet of paper and many cigarettes! All people were in right spirits and soon every man

The letter from Jannie Van Splunder to Keith Bennett thanking him, his crew and the Allies for Operation Manna . . .

was smoking! Even some girls had a cigarette which they kept as a souvenir. So had my friend Bouwine Van Vliet, who did already write to you sooner than I do, I believe. At last she and I got an opportunity to read the sheet of paper and on the railing of the viaduct both of us copied your and your friend's names. We copied them, because one of the men liked to keep the original sheet. Can you speak a little Dutch, for you wrote: Royal Australian Air Force naar U! We thought this very clever! We two agreed upon writing to you as soon as letters could be sent to Australia. That's why you get a letter from an unknown Dutch girl. I dared not write sooner to you, because I was afraid that my letter would be lost, for the circumstances near and in Indonesia are still bad, so that letters could easily be lost. I was also afraid that you had not yet returned at home. I hope you are at home now! I am sure that you are brave and nice! Here in Holland all people speak about their Allied friends with great admiration, you Australian, Canadian, American and English airmen, soldiers and are our heroes!!! We shall never, never forget all your sacrifices for our small country! I wish I could explain better to you, how much I and every Dutchman like you and all your friends!!

I do hope that you have one minute time left for me to answer me, so that I can keep your letter as a souvenir for all my life! (You see, I like notes of exclamation! I have a diary of this war and I should like it very very much if I had a picture of you, then I stick it beside the story of your aeroplane into my diary. I am afraid I am very impudent but I should be so glad with it! If you write, will you tell me what sort of thing you like as a present? You have done so much for us and my dad, mother, twin, sisters and I should think it awfully nice to give something to you. If you write, would you be so kind to tell me the adress of your friend Alby Murray, for I am afraid I copied his address wrongly. I thought he lives 116 High Street, West Maitland, N.S.W. Van Diemensland. But I believe West Maitland does not exist on Van Diemensland. Now I'll finish this very long letter and I hope that you will answer me!

Many hearty greetings from Yannie van Splunder.
What's the highest speed of your machine? Bye. b

. . . a letter that would change their war and lead to a lifelong bond.

Fun and games at university, with the 'Butchers and Greasers' procession through Sydney in 1948. Keith Bennett (back left) was proud of his masterpiece, 'Fanny by Gaslight', which adorned the left side of the truck.

Keith Bennett, with wife Elva, enjoyed a drink on his eightieth birthday at the Lane Cove Bowling Club, aka 'the Diddy'.

AUSTRALIAN AIRMAN'S BRIDE

Flight Sergeant Harold Victor Ford, R.A.A.F., and Miss Patricia Alwyn Griffiths, among their attendants on leaving St. Nicholas' Church, Brighton, after yesterday's wedding. Australian airmen formed a guard of honour as the newly-wedded pair left the church.

Guard of Honour at Brighton

MEMBERS OF THE Royal Australian Air Force formed a guard of honour at the wedding at St. Nicholas' Church, Brighton, yesterday, between Flight Sergeant Harold Victor Ford, R.A.A.F., son of Mr. and Mrs. V. H. Ford, of and carried a bouquet.

She was attended by Emmie Harvey, Mrs. Nina Griffiths (sister-in-law), and two nieces, Miss Barbara Earl and Miss Yvonne Dinery. Their dresses were of blue crepe-romaine, with headdresses of blue feathers, and they carried posies of yellow chrysanthemums. Flying Officer T. E. Emerson, a member of the bridegroom's crew, did duty as best man, and little Miss Patricia Harvey, another niece, presented the bride with a lucky horseshoe.

Harold 'Henry' Ford's wedding to Pat was not only attended by the crew of G2, but was reported in the English press.

Henry and Pat Ford today.

Elva Bennett still maintains close contact with her husband's surviving crew and their families. Here she is with Alby Murray.

Cyril Entwistle and his new
wife, Dorothy, on their wedding
day in August 1945.

Cyril Entwistle, sixty-one
years on.

Jannie Verstigen at the landmark just outside Ridderkerk where the package fell from G2 on 1 May 1945. The Lancasters came from Rotterdam (on her left) after dropping food supplies there.

One of the images from the colourful mural at the foot of the old Willemsberg bridge in Rotterdam, depicting its bombing by the Germans on 14 May 1940.

The former Binbrook air base today: gone is the sight of Lancasters readying for take-off. All that remains is the sound of cold wind and a lone Stinger from the postwar years.

The view from the former Binbrook air base to the town of Binbrook, where the church steeple acted as a beacon for returning bombers.

St Mary and St Gabriel Church in Binbrook.

Inside is a stained-glass window installed to honour the squadrons that were based at Binbrook.

The Marquis of Granby, a favourite Binbrook pub for airmen and women during World War II, today is a heritage home.

The memorial in honour of 460 Squadron at Binbrook.

One of the most respected RAAF insignia belonged to one of the most respected squadrons.

war was rapidly coming to an end.'

Suddenly Bennett was drawn to the outskirts of one town southeast of Rotterdam.

There, on a small bridge that crossed a canal, he saw a gathering of people and noticed that many were school children. Instinctively he knew that this was the mark for his and Alby's drop. On Bennett's order of 'go!', Firkins dropped the cigarettes from the plane. The crew could see people scrambling for the parcel below, but they couldn't linger. With a quick tilt of the wings – the airman's wave – they bade farewell and returned to Binbrook. As they made their return trip home, two young girls were unwrapping the contents of their package and noting down the addresses of two Australian airmen.

For Bennett and his crew, playing a role in Operation Manna was immeasurably satisfying. What a rare privilege it was to end the war saving lives rather than destroying them. As Bennett wrote in his diary after returning to Binbrook from their first food-drop: 'The whole population must have turned out to cheer us. Many people waved sheets and flags. It was a real pleasure to do such an appreciated job.'

YEAR		AIRCRAFT		Pilot, or	2nd Pilot, Pupil	DUTY
Month	Date	Type	No.	1st Pilot	or Passenger	(Including Results and Remarks)
—	—	—	—	—		---- Totals Brought Forward
MAY	3	LANCASTER III	G²	SELF	F/O EMERSON	30TH. OPERATION
					SGT ENTWISTLE	SUPPLY DROPPING NEAR
					F/S MURRAY	ROTTERDAM. 4 BLOCKS
					T/S FORD	OF 284 SACKS. 416 MLS
					T/S FREEZER	WEATHER STILL VERY
					F/S FIRKINS	SQUALLY

7. Lawrence S/L
O.C. 'C' FLIGHT

SUMMARY FOR. MAY.   TYPES.
UNIT   460 SQUADRON   LANCASTER I
DATE   5.5.45   LANCASTER III
SIGNATURE R.W. Kennett

(signature) W/C.
C.O. 460 SQUADRON.

TOTAL HOURS FOR 460 SQUADRON.

Chapter 11

Liberation

We'll meet again. Don't know where. Don't know when. But I know we'll meet again some sunny day.

Vera Lynn

LIKE MOST DUTCH, JANNIE VAN SPLUNDER had believed that Operations Manna and Chowhound heralded the long-awaited end to the pain and suffering of wartime. But as the Allies celebrated VE Day on 8 May, she and her fellow villagers at Ridderkerk were made to endure one final act of horror.

While the Allies were rejoicing, Ridderkerk's postwar calm was suddenly broken by the burst of gunfire. The Dutch Resistance was rounding up female collaborators, many of whom had willingly slept with the enemy – known as 'dishonourable fraternisation'. Later, collaborators were forced to undergo the public humiliation of a *knipceremonie* – where the guilty had their hair cut off while angry crowds jeered and mocked them.

One particularly violent encounter – on 8 May, VE Day of all days – between the Dutch Resistance and German officers, led to the deaths of twelve people. As Jannie recalls: 'There were German officers who had girls with them. The Resistance wanted to take the girls prisoner because they had been collaborators with the Germans . . . One of the officers began to shoot at several people. It was terrible.'

The tragic episodes at Ridderkerk contrasted sharply with the celebrations that had swept over Holland after Radio Herrijzend (Rising Netherlands) broadcast news of the liberation from its studio in Eindhoven. Canadian troops were welcomed in The Hague, Amsterdam and Rotterdam. Elsewhere, in Ijmuiden, the Resistance was helping the Canadians to disarm 18,000 German coastline defenders; in Berlin, the Germans capitulated; and the first Allied forces had arrived in Oslo.

Ronald Walker, war correspondent for *The News Chronicle* newspaper, was there to report first-hand the reaction of the Dutch. His report, published as a page-three lead story in the English paper's 8 May edition, was headlined: 'Laughter, tears on Amsterdam road'.

Walker was with a reconnaissance squadron of the 40th Division of the Canadian Army and filed his report soon after arriving in the town of Utrecht in the early morning of 7 May:

Driving along the long straight roads of free Holland to Canadian headquarters we found a country *en fête*. Everywhere fluttered the red, white, blue and orange of Holland. Small cottages flew flags almost as large as themselves. Everywhere people were out celebrating the German capitulation which had freed the other half of their country . . . From the side roads the people came running as the Canadian column raced up the roads. They crowded forward to leave only the narrowest lane open and pelt the armoured cars and the jeeps with flowers, flags and paper streamers . . . Behind us for miles the roads of Holland are lined with stacks of ammunition that will no longer be needed. The road from Wageningen is lined with stacks of food.

The convoy soon arrived at the outskirts of Utrecht where the crowds were so thick that the Canadian convoy had to come to a halt. As Walker wrote: 'Women and even men with tears streaming down their cheeks said over and over: "We have waited five years for you. Five years we have waited and now you are here."'

Peter Stursberg arrived in Utrecht with the first British armoured cars. Also a reporter, he was in Europe on assignment for England's *The Daily Herald* newspaper. Like Walker, he was overwhelmed by the outpouring of emotion from the Dutch upon their liberation. In his 8 May dispatch titled 'Dutch beat all for cheers', he wrote:

A cheering singing mob descended upon us and took over our vehicles. My coat was almost torn from my back and I found that there was no room in the jeep for me except on the spare tyre. A girl had her arm around my neck and a man was sitting on my knee: there were between forty and fifty persons on the jeep and trailer and more got on as we entered Utrecht.

After leaving Utrecht, Walker and his convoy then made their way to Amsterdam, a city – as he says in his 9 May dispatch – that 'has waited longer than any other European principal city for liberation'. Again, as he and the Canadian forces approached the city, they were swamped by a tidal wave of emotion as the Dutch greeted them with cries, tears and hugs of joy.

But the jubilation and excitement did not conceal the harsh reality of life for many Dutch people. Western Holland was still desperately short of food, energy resources and vital services. According to Walker: 'It is difficult amid these ecstatic surroundings to remember that there is a façade which hides a stark background . . . There is no gas, electricity or coal. The wood blocks have been taken from the streets by people desperate for fires, for cooking and obtaining some little warmth in the depth of winter.'

His observations are corroborated by Peter Stursberg, who wrote that behind the ear-piercing celebration of joy, the reality of Dutch suffering was starkly present: 'The effect of starvation is noticeable in the pinched faces of the people. Some are so weak from hunger they can hardly wave to us. I talked to the leader of the Resistance movement here and he told me that there was so little food people were going round from house to house begging for a potato.'

Back in Rotterdam, Pieter Oud, from a middle-class family and the son of a tobacco and wine trader, was re-instated as mayor after relinquishing the position in the autumn of 1941. Meanwhile, those among the Dutch who had collaborated with the Germans continued to be arrested. As a result of the liberation, 750 Jews felt safe enough to come out of hiding, while another 1000 returned to their home city from various camps across Europe. This was a negligible amount given how vibrant the Jewish community had been before the war. As a consequence of the community's devastation, many Jewish survivors never returned to the port city, opting instead to find new lives in the United States or Israel.

Step by step, normal life began to resume in Holland, but it was not easy. The Dutch were faced with the mammoth task of reconstructing the many buildings and infrastructure that had been destroyed by the Germans. With materials still in limited supply and the country so poor, this was a daunting task. Slowly, food supply started to regulate, services and facilities began to improve, and even entertainment and sport resumed.

But though hostilities had ceased in Europe, the war in the Pacific against Japan remained unresolved. Because this front involved the Dutch East Indies (now known as Indonesia) Dutch input was required. The call to arms was well heeded and thousands of Dutch men and women queued up to enlist. People everywhere wanted to help bring the war to an end.

For Jannie and her friend Bouwine Van Vliet, a bright future once again beckoned. Amidst the celebration of liberation, they had not forgotten the Lancaster bombers and their food-drop.

Like many Dutch people who expressed their gratitude to the Allied airmen in letters, Jannie and Bouwine wrote emotionally charged letters to the two crew members in the Lancaster, Flying Officer Keith Bennett and Flight Sergeant Alby Murray.

The first letter Bennett received was from Bouwine, who had by this time returned to her home in Rotterdam. Dated 3 December 1945, it reads:

Dear Flying Grocer

At the 1st of May 1945 I was in a village in the neighbourhood of Rotterdam. I stayed there with the parents of my girlfriend who had asked me if I wanted to come to them because they had much more food than my parents in Rotterdam.

In Rotterdam it was more than terrible. My mother was ill from hunger and the other members of our family were nearly ill. Perhaps you can understand what it was for us when we saw our friends with food! Food! Food! We cried for joy and we danced when we saw the helping aeroplanes. The whole day we were very glad and thankful to you who were so close when you saved us.

At a quarter to 5 my friend and I stood on a viaduct to wave to each aeroplane and then your plane came very low and dropped a bag with 200 cigarettes. It is a pity that you could not see the pleasure from all the people.

With trouble I could make myself master one cigarette. The brand 'Kool' was very good said my father. At first I wanted to keep the cigarette as a remembrance to you but when I came home and I heard that my father had not smoked for several weeks I gave it to him.

With the cigarettes there was a piece of paper with yours and that of your friend's addresses. It is a great pleasure for me to write to you now and to thank you for the help to our country especially to my hungry family in Rotterdam. I hope that you are now at home and that you are well. Lastly, I will ask you if you will send me a letter or a postcard as a souvenir.

Many good wishes from one of your friends in Holland.

Bouwine Van Vliet (19 years old)

Jannie Van Splunder's letter came soon after. It is dated 22 February 1946:

Dear Australian airman,

You'll probably be astonished when you get this letter from somebody who is quite unknown to you. So first I'll tell you who I am. I am a Dutch girl, nineteen years old, and I live at Ridderkerk. I wanted to write to you to tell you how grateful we are to you and your fellow flyers for all you have done for us! Last year your aeroplanes dropped innumerable boxes full of delicious food on Holland and you saved us from starving. In those days we were almost crazy with joy and excitement and everyone waved and screamed at the huge machines which often flew so low that we could see the pilot. The cruel Germans looked on very angrily at the running and crying people, but this time they dared not say a word, which was very seldom the case!

One day, a group of aeroplanes came rushing over our village and one of them (your machine!) dropped a packet! It fell down near the viaduct over the main road from Rotterdam to Dordrecht. Some people said that they had seen a flying man wave a white handkerchief. Was that you? We gazed in amazement after the big aeroplane and then we saw that it greeted us, for it heeled over from one side to the other! In our language this is called 'de vliegergroet': the airman's greeting. And then we ran and pushed and cried, till at last a man could get hold of the parcel. He unpacked a white box and it contained a sheet of paper and many cigarettes! Everyone was in highest spirits and soon every man was smoking! Even some girls had cigarettes which they kept as a souvenir. So had my friend Bouwine Van Vliet who did already write to you sooner than I do, I believe. At last she and I got an opportunity to read the sheet of paper and on the railing of the viaduct both of us copied your and your friend's names. We copied them because one of the men liked to keep the original sheet. Can you speak a little Dutch, for you write: Royal Australian Air Force *Naar U* ['To you']! We thought this very clever! We two agreed upon writing to you as soon as letters could be sent to Australia. That's why you get a letter from an unknown Dutch girl. I dared not write sooner to you because I was afraid that my letter would be lost, for circumstances near and in Indonesia are still bad, so that letters could easily be lost. I was also afraid that you had not yet returned home. I hope you are at home now! I am sure that you are brave and nice! Here in Holland people speak about their Allied friends with great admiration, you Australians, Canadian, American and English airmen, soldiers and seamen are our heroes! We shall never, never forget all your sacrifices for our small country! I wish I could explain better to you how much I and every Dutchman like you and all your friends!! I do hope that you have one minute to answer me, so that I can keep your letter as a souvenir for all my life! (You see, I like notes of exclamation). I have a diary of this war and I would like it very, very much if I had a picture of you then I would stick it beside the story of your aeroplane into my diary. I am afraid I am very impudent but I should be so glad with it! If you write will you tell me what sort of thing you will like as a present? You have done so much for us and dad, mother, twin sisters and I should think it awfully nice to give something to you. If you write would you be so kind to tell me the address of your friend Alby Murray, for I am afraid I copied his address wrongly. I thought he lives at 116 High Street West Maitland, NSW Van Diemensland. But I believe West Maitland does not exist in Van Diemensland. Now I'll finish this very long letter and I hope that you will answer me!

Many hearty greetings from Jannie Van Splunder

What's the highest speed of your machine? Bye-bye.

In Jannie's next letter to Bennett – dated 1 May 1946, the anniversary of their parcel-drop over the viaduct at Ridderkerk – she explains how 1 May had become a national memorial day for those killed in the war. The country was ablaze with Dutch national flags flying half-mast. Jannie also detailed the day's activities in Ridderkerk, and the Allied tribute to the Queen in memory of the start of Operation Manna:

We have just returned home from the cemetery. The clergyman of our village who had been a prisoner of the 'Tofs' [Germans] conducted the memorial service on the graves of the Ridderkerk soldiers. First a captain of the infantry laid down a big wreath of lilacs and arum lilies with a red, white and blue ribbon around them. After that the minister said a very beautiful prayer. How solemn it was with the poplars high in the very blue sky and it was so silent. When the prayer was finished we sang the national anthem: 'The Wilhelmus'. And then everybody returned home. At 8 o'clock there was a service in the church with a male choir singing appropriate songs. Tomorrow is the day of festivals. Then everybody is glad and there will be fireworks and processions and public games. From 11–12 o'clock all schools will commemorate the liberation ....

Last Monday a Lancaster came with flowers for our Queen. It dropped them on the aerodrome of Soesterberg [the Dutch Air Force base near Utrecht liberated by Canadian forces in May 1945], not far from the palace of the Prince and Princess where the Queen was a guest that day. This was as a remembrance of 29 April last year when the Allied forces came with food for the first time.

Vele groeten van [signed] Jannie

PS: We have the Australian national anthem and we often play and sing it.

As well as letters from Bouwine and Jannie, Alby Murray received letters of gratitude from men who felt compelled to express their thanks to the Australian airmen. One such letter is from Theo Van Straten, also from Ridderkerk, and a recipient of their cigarette package. Dated 1 January 1948, it reads:

Dear Sir

You will be surprised to read something from Ridderkerk as you have never been there before – at least not with your knowledge.

Ridderkerk is a village in Holland situated on the island of Yselmonde between the towns of Rotterdam and Dordrecht. Although you have never been in our village you have flown over us with food-stuffs and we called you good people the 'flying grocers'.

Looking through an old wallet of mine today I found a piece of paper on which was your address and also that of some of your friends . . . This piece of paper, attached to the crown of an old hat, together with a parcel of 200 cigarettes, was dropped out of your plane above the bridge over the highway to Ridderkerk. It is a pity that you were not there on earth to see the joy with which those cigarettes were divided and the quick way they disappeared in smoke. Having been for such a long time without a smoke, the cigarettes were indeed very much appreciated, and we have never tasted a cigarette after that day with such a nice flavour and aroma.

All the Ridderkerkers thank you very much for all the good you have done for us in Holland.

Yours truly

S. Th. Van Straten

Another letter was written by Aafje Verschoor from the town of Slikkerveer. He was also on the viaduct near Ridderkerk when Bennett and Murray flew over the town after dropping food supplies over Rotterdam on 1 May. Dated 19 January 1948, it reads:

Dear Alby Murray

It is now a year since I found your address. Yes, it was a funny business, but before I proceed I would like to introduce myself.

My name is Aafje Verschoor and I live in Slikkerveer, though I was born in Rotterdam. When I was six years old my mother died and since then I have lived with my uncle and aunt as a foster child. I have two sisters who live with their father in Rotterdam. I was born in 1930 and I am now 16 years of age. I work in the office of Klavarkribe of which you probably might have heard. It is a music institute.

As I said above, it was a funny business with the result that it gave us a lot of joy – how much I cannot tell you, for you must experience it yourself before you can really understand it as hunger is something terrible.

Now I will tell you something about how I got your address. We were standing near the bridge and it was very bad weather with a lot of rain but we didn't feel anything of that as we had to look for the aeroplanes that were coming. It was a marvellous spectacle – all those aeroplanes – but not only that, for over Rotterdam we saw all the food parcels coming down and we knew we would have something to eat.

The people were mad with joy – they danced and jumped around and waved, which is not surprising because at that time we were living on one plate of cabbage soup per day and had to work on that. It was terrible to be hungry for such a long time as we were, but I cannot tell you everything about that as I would not have enough paper.

Well, we were standing near the bridge with another twenty people when a flyer came very low and we saw something like a white cloth in front of the cockpit. What happened next I do not know, but all the people ran down the embankment, made a lot of noise and cried because very soon we found a jute bag with contents. The man who picked up the bag opened up the parcel and there were cigarettes in it which disappeared very soon in smoke and I must admit that we forgot about all the aeroplanes until all the cigarettes were divided up. You realise that there were so many men there that there was nothing left for us.

We looked around for a while until a boy came along with a paper with your address. I have not written up to now as I thought that probably you would still be in service. As you will be at home now I suppose, I have taken pen to paper to write and thank you for the pleasant day you gave us.

I would be very pleased if you could drop us a little note because we are all so very curious to know who helped us, and all my boy and girl friends have asked me to thank you very much for the work you have done for us in Holland.

Aafje Verschoor,

Slikkerveer

～

The war may have stolen five precious years of Jannie's teens, but in its aftermath, romance was not far away.

The Verstigens in Rotterdam were friends of Jannie's parents. Realising the extent of the suffering in the port city, Henri and Wilhelmina Van Splunder used to share with the

Verstigens whatever food they could spare. When the war was over, the Verstigens' son Gerrit visited Ridderkerk to thank the Van Splunders, and give them a book as a token of their appreciation. On that day, Gerrit met Jannie for the first time, sparking immediate interest on both sides.

Though 'love was in the air', Jannie and Gerrit were separated when she decided to travel with Bouwine to London, where the two girls worked as au pairs. Jannie really enjoyed her spell in England, as she told Bennett in a letter: 'I saw and enjoyed a good deal and enjoyed London and the beautiful English coast as we had holidays in Sussex and Devon.' She admits that returning home was not simple: 'It is a bit difficult now to get used to everything in Holland again, as our country is quite different from England.'

In the same letter, she speaks of the political differences brewing between Australia and Holland over Indonesia (formerly the Dutch East Indies) as outlined in a newspaper cutting he had mailed to her. She writes:

It is true that Australia is not so popular in Holland which is partly your former government's fault with its attitude with respect to the Dutch affairs in Indonesia. Our weak Labour government has spoilt everything now, so that Indonesia is no longer ours. We are furious about it, not because we don't want the Dutch Indies to be independent, but because we don't like the way in which it happened. It really brings a blush to our cheeks. But the article says there is a startling lack of real knowledge about Australia. This is also true. Lots of people hardly know anything about your far country; it is one of the least-known countries for us, as it is still rather young. You will know yourself that the Australian government does not give admittance to immigrants very often. We know that doctors, farmers and technicians have a fairly good chance, but people with other professions a very poor one. Moreover, one has to go with some capital, and then British people and even displaced persons I believe have priority. I learnt just now that a boy who was in my form in the elementary school and had to go to Indonesia as a soldier is going to Australia as soon as he leaves the army. He is a farmer's son so probably he will be able to earn a good living there.

The interest in Australia, Jannie explains in her letter to Bennett, was partly due to the difficulties of postwar life in Holland, especially for rural people:

At the moment it is terribly difficult for the farmers in Holland to earn their living as there is so much industrialisation everywhere. Our village is getting overpopulated, also because there is a great lack of materials to build houses. There are about 800 people in Ridderkerk now who wait for a house of their own. All of them are living with their relations or even with complete strangers, which is an untenable position, of course.

Our country is getting poorer and poorer and I am sure that emigration will increase even more, perhaps to Australia too, when conditions become better gradually.

While in England, Jannie also wrote to Gerrit Verstigen. However, it was only once she returned home to Holland that she and Gerrit began dating each other officially. Five years after the war ended, in 1950, the two got married.

In the years that followed, the flow of letters between Jannie and Keith Bennett grew less frequent and eventually dried up. Divided by distance and caught up in new lives with their young families, the fall-off in communication is understandable.

Contact between the two families resumed in the 1980s when Bennett contacted the Van Splunder family hoping to track down Jannie. He had planned a visit to the Netherlands and was keen to meet Jannie face to face.

In 1985, following the celebrations commemorating the fortieth anniversary of the food-drop, Jannie again wrote to Bennett and described her impressions of the occasion. Twenty-four planes flew en masse over Rotterdam and Amsterdam, Hilversum and Laren on their way to the military base at Loesterberg. The Dutch, Royal, Australian and Canadian airforces were all represented, and the range of planes that flew over her homeland were many and varied. Jannie writes of her regret that Bennett was not among those airforce veterans who attended:

It was exactly forty years ago today that Allied aeroplanes dropped food packages in Holland's cities. I got a lump in my throat when I saw those old-fashioned aeroplanes fly very low and solid over our village and thought of the day you dropped a parcel with cigarettes over the Ridderkerk viaduct. The Lancaster seems to be the only Lancaster in the world which is able to fly still. We had understood and hoped you would have been one of the 200 or so flyers who came to Holland with their wives to commemorate Operation Manna. After forty years we want to express once more our gratefulness for your self-sacrifice in great danger so that we can live in freedom now.

Year		Aircraft		Pilot, or 1st Pilot	2nd Pilot, Pupil or Passenger	Duty (Including Results and Remarks)
Month	Date	Type	No.			
—	—	—	—	—	—	Totals Brought Forward
May	3	Lancaster III	G2	Self	F/o Emerson	30th. Operation
					Sgt. Entwistle	Supply dropping near
					F/s Murray	Rotterdam. 4 Blocks
					T/s Ford	of 284 sacks. 416 mls
					T/s Freezer	Weather still very
					F/s Firkins	squally

F. Lawrence S/L
O.C. 'C' Flight

[signature] W/C.
C.O. 460 Squadron.

Summary for May.
Unit   460 Squadron
Date   5.5.45
Signature   [signature]

Types.
Lancaster I
Lancaster III

Total Hours For 460 Squadron.

Chapter 12

Victory At Last

*After five years, eight months and four days of the
bloodiest war in history, Britain and her Allies have
gained victory in Europe.*

London's *The Daily Mirror*, 8 May 1945

FOLLOWING GERMANY'S SURRENDER, the whole of Europe celebrated; elation was the dominant mood – as it was at Binbrook,
where those airmen who survived the war were excitedly planning their journeys home. But the celebrations at the Village Inn
were tempered by a keen awareness of those among them who
did not make it to the end. In addition, many struggled to come
to terms with the sudden change that had swept over their lives.
'As far as we were concerned, when the war ended it was an
anti-climax,' recalls Bennett's flight engineer, Cyril Entwistle.
Suddenly not having to anticipate an operation left a void,
despite its inherent dangers. As he explains:

There we were: up for flights being decided in the morning, waiting there to see if your name is on the battle order, and when it is your adrenalin starts flowing, and suddenly it's all over – all at once. There you are the next week and you think, 'I've got nothing to look forward to anymore.' It's a queer sort of thing. In a sense it is a weight off your mind. You haven't got to worry about going to the pub and [wondering if you will be] having a drink tomorrow night. You know you can do it.

Of course, the end of the war did not come overnight. Even before Operations Manna and Chowhound were carried out, all indicators pointed towards an Allied victory. This mood of confidence is clear in Bennett's diary – if not by its buoyant tone, then by the increasing length and regularity of his entries. As each entry indicates, Bennett and his fellow servicemen were excited by their imminent return home and relieved to see the end of such a horribly tragic period of world history. Furthermore, they were looking forward to once again enjoying the simple pleasures that war had taken away – from catching a replay of the 1945 Melbourne Cup, to dancing in open streets without the fear of a German bombing raid, and again relishing the pleasures of ice-cream – then a luxury.

Bennett also mentions being advised that all sorties in Operation Manna would be officially recognised as operational flights – indicating the regard with which the mission was held by Bomber Command.

Following is a sample of his diary entries from this time.

Wednesday, 2 May
Hitler is supposed to be dead. German radio announced his death in the Berlin Chancellery – fighting Bolshevism. Not flying today. Special newsreel of the Melbourne Cup shown for our benefit – gratis.

Friday, 4 May
The Air Force decided to count 'spam' trips [as] ops and screen us. So Les, Henry, Alby, Cyril and I got screaming in Binbrook village.

Saturday, 5 May
News today – All Hun forces surrender in NW Germany, Holland and Denmark. Spent day getting log-book finished and preparing for leave.

Monday, 7 May
Got ready to leave this morning, but before we could clear up, this transport command business had to be cleared up. Could have gone myself to 'Halibags'. The result, we missed the early London trains and stopped in G.Y for this night. Tomorrow is to be V day, it was announced this evening.

Tuesday, 8 May
Les [Emmerson] caught the 5.20 train and I missed it to London. Eventually arrived about lunchtime at the Boomerang Club. V Day was well away. Crowds of AIF POWs were having a lively time around Australia House. Organised myself for a party starting at 4.30. After eating ice-cream all afternoon, travelled to Highgate. Three more Aussies came and we had a nice time with light drink. Every street corner had its little bonfire and we danced from one to another at midnight. Searchlights gave a display too. The result was that I've caught a beaut cold.

The cheer that erupted as VE Day was announced – in London and throughout Europe – was thunderous. On 8 May, the front-page headline of the English newspaper *The Daily Herald* read: 'Good morning! This is VE-Day (official) – Europe at Peace.' Meanwhile, in another newspaper, *The Daily Sketch* from Kemsley, the page-one headline declared: 'This is VE-Day – Prime Minister to announce the end in Europe this afternoon'. Inside ran a two-page photo-spread illustrating the contrasting fates of the Allies and the Germans. Indicating Allied success was a picture of the 5th Battalion Grenadier Guards at Wellington Barracks in their march past Princess Elizabeth, Colonel of the regiment; an open-air battlefield lunch at Torgeau to celebrate the historic link-up of American and Russian forces; smiling ATS (Auxiliary Territorial Service) members boarding planes bound for Brussels to work with British ground forces on the Continent; and pigeons being fed British army rations at San Marco Square in Venice. Indicating German misfortune, two photos showed U-boats being attacked and sunk by Mosquitoes from RAF Coastal Command, and one depicted forlorn German officers under escort as they arrived in London to be confronted by a mass of victory flags. In its special 'Victory Issue', *The News Chronicle* newspaper ran the official announcement:

> It is understood that, in accordance with arrangements between the three Great Powers, an official announcement will be made by the Prime Minister at three o'clock tomorrow afternoon, May 8. In view of this fact, tomorrow, Tuesday, will be treated as Victory in Europe Day

and will be regarded as a holiday. The following day, 9 May will also be a holiday. His Majesty the King will broadcast to the peoples of the British Empire and Commonwealth tomorrow at 9 pm. Parliament will meet at the usual time tomorrow.

Details of the complete and unconditional surrender by the Germans were also reported. The German foreign minister Lutz Scherwin Von Krosigk had made the announcement the previous day in an afternoon broadcast; it was signed at 2.41 am on 8 May by the chief-of-staff of the German army, Colonel General Alfred Jodl, in a small red schoolhouse in Reims, which had been General Dwight Eisenhower's latest headquarters.

Eisenhower did not attend the formal surrender, but representing the Allied powers were General Bedell-Smith for the United States and Britain, General Ivan Suslaparov for the Soviet Union, and General François Sevez for France. According to *The News Chronicle*:

'The German emissaries were repeatedly asked: "Do you understand the significance of the seriousness of these terms?" The Germans replied that they did. When the signing was complete General Jodl said: "With this signature the German people and the German armed forces are, for better or for worse, delivered into the victors' hands."'

As the euphoria of VE Day continued to sweep across London – and the whole of England – hundreds of thousands of people made their way to Buckingham Palace where, after a two-hour wait during which they chanted 'We want the King!', the crowd was treated to the first of eight Royal appearances on the Palace balcony, which was draped in crimson and gold material. The Queen appeared, dressed in pale blue and wearing a hat; the King was wearing his Navy Admiral's uniform; Princess Margaret wore military khaki; and Princess Elizabeth was in blue like her mother yet without a hat. Over the next hours as they appeared, disappeared and appeared again, the Royals answered the public's cheers with waves and kisses.

An hour after the Royal Family's first appearance on the balcony, word spread that Prime Minister Churchill would shortly arrive to meet the Royal Family. The moment came, with Churchill sitting in his open car preceded by six mounted policemen. Those who were close enough reported seeing tears roll down the great man's cheeks as he looked to the crowds that lined every inch of his passage until he was through the Palace gates. In the words of an eyewitness, the people were awaiting 'the greatest moment of all'.

Soon enough, the Palace doors slowly opened again and the crowd madly cheered the man who had just led them to victory. As he came out to stand alongside the Royal Family, Churchill offered no wave to the crowd, nor his customary two-fingered V for victory sign. As was reported in *The News Chronicle*:

He simply stood there, his head slightly bowed. And the scores of thousands who looked up at him and at the King, the Queen and Princesses seemed to hold their breath, to be completely still and silent for an unforgettable moment. This was the proudest happiest moment of all who waited. And this, surely, was the greatest, proudest, most unforgettable of all the mighty moments in the life of Winston Churchill.

Then Churchill bowed in a gesture of recognition of the people's support and courage through the long years of war. And as abruptly as the cheers had come to a halt when he and the Royals first stood before them, the crowd erupted again and pressed against the Palace gates. Later, at the Ministry of Health in Whitehall, Churchill and his cabinet presented themselves before a crowd of 50,000. Once again, he was greeted with a jubilant cheer. *The News Chronicle* later reported: 'This was his day.' But Churchill thought otherwise. For later in a speech to the people, he told them: 'This is your victory.'

One of the most poignant images of VE Day in London was the sight of St Paul's Cathedral bathed under a flood of light soon after sunset. Readers were reminded that the last time it appeared 'lit up' was on 29 December 1940 during the 'great fire raid on London' when the cathedral was enveloped in flames and smoke. Elsewhere in London on VE Day, giant wartime searchlights spot-lit all the monuments of the English capital, expressing renewed strength and pride – from Buckingham Palace, London Tower, and Westminster Palace where the Union Jack flew at full-mast, to Lord Nelson on his column and the National Gallery in Trafalgar Square. The euphoria that had swept across London – and all of England – throughout the day continued as people partied on well into the night. They danced in the streets; they climbed lightposts, statues and monuments to get a better view of the spectacles of celebration.

The atmosphere of VE Day was aptly captured by A.J. Cummings in a page-one story for *The News Chronicle*. Cummings could not help but make the comparison between the festive mood he was now experiencing and the apprehension, restlessness and deadly calm of a night in September 1939 when war with Germany seemed imminent. In a story headlined: 'Not one unhappy face in the vast throngs' he wrote:

The contrast was striking enough. There was gaiety in the air, a conscious sense of release from strain. I did not see an unhappy face in these vast, orderly throngs of people. They were not noisy. There were little pools of noise among the young soldiers on leave, arm-in-arm with their girls. There were little processions of young men and women with flags and rattles and many coloured caps just letting themselves go in the joy of the moment. But generally speaking, these hundreds of thousands of people from every walk of life, who moved towards the familiar centres of London life and then stood and sat wherever they could find a seat for hours on end, watching the scene and one another, were very much like what one always expects a London crowd to be. I have seen immense congregations of peoples in many of the great capitals of the world. But a rejoicing London crowd is unique in its self-discipline, its orderliness, its good humour, its unconquerable patience and its intimacy. It was a thoroughly happy experience to become one of the great army that assembled in front of Buckingham Palace. There they were, in their scores of thousands, young and old, Guards officers and their wives, men on leave with their sweethearts, elderly couples whose sons were in France or in Burma or on the sea. Wrens, girls of the ATS, English sailors, a sprinkling of American boys, trimly dressed business men, office girls in groups – a recognisable cross-section of a great community.

As a journalist on assignment, Cummings spent a lot of his time talking to people on the streets. He realised that not a single person he spoke to had avoided any suffering as a result of the war. He ended his story by capturing three lasting impressions:

A sudden hush in Trafalgar Square as the clear voice of Field Marshal Montgomery came through the loud-speaker giving thanks for victory. The unusual sight of a majestic sergeant of police platonically kissing two young women who waved flags in his face. Finally, the thrilling spectacle of St Paul's floodlit. The great west front had a strange look of ethereal translucence and the glowing white cross above the dome shone down upon London at peace.

Following VE Day, Bennett – freed of the stress and life-threatening risks of wartime – made use of the downtime by travelling the country that had become his adopted home. He visited English relatives, enjoyed evenings at various pubs, and saw films in re-opened cinemas. His diary entries read:

Wednesday, 9 May

Caught an early train to Birmingham, arriving about 7.30 pm. Celebrated with a quiet 'noggin' at the Red Lion.

Thursday, 10 May

A sleep-in to get over V Day etc. and the Red Lion.

Sunday, 13 May

Saw Anne Hathaway's cottage, also Howard House, Shakespeare's house and Memorial theatre. A showery but very enjoyable day.

Monday, 14 May

Went with Paddy to see a very good picture: A Song to Remember at the Odeon.

Tuesday, 15 May

A short afternoon walk to Handsworth Park and then the Newsagents Dinner at The Red Lion. Got a bit full.

Wednesday, 16 May

Shopping with auntie 'Lil'. Bought mum and her a length of dress material. This evening we went to the local cinema with [cousin] Jill and uncle Bill to see Shine on Harvest Moon – okay too.

Saturday, 19 May

A boat and another train brought me to Belfast at about 11 am. Fixed myself up at the Canadian Legions for tonight. Chummed up with a couple of Aussies at the Officers' Club and we went to a Honky Tonk dance this evening. Bags of bags!

Sunday, 20 May

A wet and miserable day – feeling a bit fed up with bally Belfast. May go back to Birmingham. Saw picture: 30 seconds over Tokyo today.

Getting home to Australia was a difficult and time-consuming challenge that could take up to six months as ships were full of returned servicemen and particularly prisoners of war. Hence, many servicemen took the opportunity to travel around England. But the frustration of not knowing the immediate future got to Bennett and his crew, who had not yet parted ways. Indeed, as his diary entries show, they even contemplated further service.

Monday, 28 May

Left for camp this morning via London. Couldn't get much guts at Kodak House as to when we were going home.

Tuesday, 29 May

Station is pretty dull – only cross country flying on. A long range Lancs squadron is being formed to go out east. Don't think I'll volunteer though! Crew want me to go except Les [Emmerson] who'll be getting out when we get home.

In the aftermath of the war – and with plenty of spare time on their hands – there was plenty of debate among the servicemen about military honours – who deserved them, who would get them, who wouldn't or shouldn't. Bennett bet on and against himself being awarded a Distinguished Flying Cross (DFC) – though it seems he hedged his betting both ways:

Wednesday, 30 May
[Name withheld] has received the immediate DFC for B-all. A couple of others have it too. Wouldn't stop on squadron for anything. Pleased to see Bruce Haffer back from POW. No news of Geoff Holmes yet.

Monday, 25 June
Spent all day getting cleared, will be moving on Thursday. Laid 5 to 3 Pounds to me getting a DFC with F/Lt Bromley. Also an even 5/- with F/O Whitehead [that] I don't get one as well as Stg1 with Pete.

Unbeknown to Bennett at the time, his superiors at both the Binbrook airbase and at Bomber Command headquarters had already recommended him for the third highest military award in the RAAF. Later that year, when Bennett was finally en route back to Australia, his parents received the official cable announcing his honour. His father was excited as anyone when the ship Bennett travelled home on docked at Woolloomooloo. After Bennett and his fellow returned servicemen disembarked, his father – with his youngest son Alan next to him in the passenger's seat – followed them in his 1920 Chevy.

The journey took them to Bradfield Park where Bennett's

military service began in September 1942, but this time he was transferred there by bus to be officially discharged.

Bennett's decoration was also announced in the 6 November edition of *The London Gazette*, where he was listed as one of eighteen RAAF servicemen awarded DFCs, four of whom were from the much decorated 460 Squadron that earned 228 DFCs in the war.

The recommendations from his three commanding officers were as follows:

F/O Bennett is an Australian pilot who has completed his first tour of 30 operations with Bomber Command. These included attacks on heavily defended targets at Hanover, Essen (2), Dortmund, Bremen (2) and Mannheim. This officer's tour has been dominated by the desire to bomb the enemy at all costs, regardless of personal safety, as evidenced on the night of 21 February 1945, in an attack on Duisburg. Before target the aircraft was hit by flak and the starboard outer engine was put out of action, but despite this F/O Bennett proceeded to the target and bombed successfully on three engines. On return he landed at an emergency airfield on two engines due to broken fuel line putting the starboard engines out of action. F/O Bennett's whole tour of operations has been characterised by exceptional qualities of leadership and coolness and is possessed with a fine offensive spirit which has earned him the admiration of all members of the squadron. In recognition of his fine record, consistent gallantry and devotion to duty, I recommend the award of the Distinguished Flying Cross

Wing Commander Michael George Cowan, 13 May 1945

F/O Bennett, though naturally of a quiet and retiring disposition, has shown a fine spirit in action which has inspired his crew's confidence and enabled them to achieve an outstanding record. In the face of heavy odds he always showed courage and coolness of the highest order and his determination to press home each attack inspired all other members of the squadron. I recommend that this officer's fine record be recognised by the award of the Distinguished Flying Cross.

Binbrook station commander Group Captain Keith Parsons,
14 May 1945

Strongly recommended for the non-immediate award of the Distinguished Flying Cross.

Air officer commanding No. 1 Group, Air Vice Marshal
M.G Simmons, 23 May 1945

460 Squadron's final parade was at East Kirkby (where the squadron had moved to join No. 5 Group as a part of Tiger Force and to train for the war against Japan). But that training was called off on 17 August after the Japanese surrender. *The Australian Women's Weekly* was at that final parade to capture the moment on 4 October, 1945 and in the 17 November 1945 edition published in detail the last significant chapter in the

distinguished history of the squadron, which officially disbanded on 10 October. In her article headlined 'Famous Squadron disbands, but its legend remains', the magazine's London staff writer Hazel Jackson recalls the words of the Wing Commander Peter H. Swan DSO, DFC – who had made the squadron's last flight two days earlier to Amiens to collect photos of the Australian War Memorial which honoured the First A.I.F – as his men lined up for parade at the dispersal unit: '"Righto boys, last halt for the squadron," he orders with grin.'

Then, according to Jackson, with 'a sharp order, a slash of boots, a smart salute', 460 Squadron 'had taken the first step on the road home' to Australia. By 25 October, all members of the squadron had been ordered to Gamston for repatriation back home.

The following extract from her story captures the mood and meaning of the day:

Giant Lancasters, looming through the fog like prehistoric monsters, formed a surrealistic backdrop for the final parade. The whole station turned out in honour for the squadron. To the strains of 'Advance Australia' from the RAF band, the air officer commanding RAAF overseas headquarters, Air Vice-Marshal H.N Wrigley, CBE, DFC, AFC, accompanied by the commanding officer of the squadron W/Cdr Peter Swan, DSO, DFC and Bar, and senior officers of the RAF moved slowly through the ranks. There were plenty of highly decorated men in those ranks. Following the inspection, the commanding officer of the station, Group-captain Carey, read a brief summary of the squadron's record. And a most impressive record it is. It has taken part in all the major bombing operations over Italy, Germany and France, first in Wellingtons, later in Lancasters. It formed part of the 'thousand bomber raids' of 1942, made 6264 sorties, has dropped 34,856 tonnes of bombs and has flown 4,788,582 operational miles. After a brief address by the base air commander and Air Vice-Marshal Wrigley, the parade moved off past the saluting base, and the long line of blue and grey vanished into the fog. I could not quite believe that I had seen that parade. For so long we in Australia had read about the exploits of these men and thrilled to the news of them that the squadron had almost attained the impersonality of a legend. Now I watched the completion of the legend. With their aircraft around them they had said their farewell, and then, like the Knights of King Arthur, the fog swallowed them. The men of the squadron will go their separate ways, but the legend remains.

After the parade, Jackson visited many of the squadron members in the sergeants' mess hall. They spoke little of themselves, she noted. That night, she attended a dance at the officers' mess to farewell all the officers of 460 Squadron. Also there were WAAF officers who had worked and danced alongside the male officers of 460 Squadron since their arrival in England, and many RAF members who had fought alongside them during bombing operations. The emotion of the occasion was high, and it clearly struck a chord with Jackson, who wrote:

> The RAAF seem sorry to say good-bye to the many friends they have made over here, but the magic words 'home for Christmas' have provided an undercurrent of excitement for days. The disbandment of '460' means more than the fact these men are going home. A squadron is not just the men who fly the planes, or even the men who happen to be posted there at any one time. It is all the men who have ever served there, and all the things they stand for – courage, good fellowship, hard, dogged work – built into a structure greater than them all. The reputation of this squadron stands as a symbol of all that Australians have done in this war. Some of them did not live to see the finish. As one man said to me, referring to a well-deserved DFC: 'This belongs to five other blokes.'

> The disbandment of '460' means that the task all those 'other blokes' were helping with is finished in honour. The world is free to go forward to new things, and – the boys are coming home!

YEAR		AIRCRAFT		Pilot, or 1st Pilot	2nd Pilot, Pupil or Passenger	DUTY (Including Results and Remarks)
Month	Date	Type	No.			
—	—	—	—	—	—	—— Totals Brought Forward
MAY	3	LANCASTER III	G²/2	SELF	F/O EMERSON	30TH. OPERATION
					SGT ENTWISTLE	SUPPLY DROPPING NEAR
					F/S MURRAY	ROTTERDAM. 4 BLOCKS
					T/S FORD	OF 284 SACKS. 416 MLS
					F/S FREEZER	WEATHER STILL. VERY
					F/S FIRKINS	SQUALLY

F. Lawrence S/L
OC. 'C' FLIGHT

[signature] W/C.
C.O. 460 SQUADRON.

SUMMARY FOR. MAY   TYPES.
UNIT   460 SQUADRON   LANCASTER I
DATE   5·5·45   LANCASTER III
SIGNATURE   [signature]

TOTAL HOURS FOR 460 SQUADRON.

Chapter 13

Living Again

We said all that, made the promises [to meet up again]; but it never happened.

Henry Ford

IN JANNIE VAN SPLUNDER'S FIRST LETTER to the Australian airmen, she asked what they would like as a present, as a gesture of her gratitude. Yet as is clear from Keith Bennett's reply, Jannie's correspondence and the memories of that marvellous mission were more than enough of a reward. As he wrote to her on 22 March 1946: 'Thank you very much for wanting to send a present, but please don't. I feel fully rewarded by your nice letter. We put our addresses on the parcel in the hope someone would write and let us know how successful our flights were.' He added that her letter 'will always be one of my most treasured possessions'.

Despite his mental scars from the war, Bennett maintained his ties with the services – or at least with those who served.

After returning from the war in late 1945, Bennett and his younger brother Jack – who flew Kittyhawk fighter planes in the Pacific in the war against Japan – were happy young men, appreciative of the chance to resume their lives when so many of their colleagues were either dead or disabled from the war; indeed, both felt very lucky to have escaped as they did.

Back in Australia, they enjoyed new-found independence, but it was still limited to a degree because of their father. As they still lived in the family home, Bennett snr imposed a midnight curfew on the pair. And failure to abide by it earned a simple but effective penalty: the household would be locked and they would have to sleep on the home veranda or in the workshop. His father's discipline may have appeared too overbearing, especially considering his son was now a war veteran and not the innocent teenager who left the family home in 1942 when he enlisted in the services. But there was no denying the pride he felt for his son, whose service officially came to an end on 7 January 1946. And on no better occasion did he get to show it than when Bennett received the Distinguished Flying Cross, as well as the 1939–45 Star, France and Germany Star and Defence Medal. For it was Bennett snr – a highly regarded World War I pilot in his own right and an RAAF Air Training Corps Squadron Leader during World War II – who was given the honour of presenting the DFC to him.

The boys joined an association whose aim was to welcome home ex-servicemen and women, and it was at their first meeting, held in 1946 at Lane Cove School of Arts, that Keith met Elva Pittaway, the daughter of a stonemason, who would become his wife. As she recalls, 'Most of us knew somebody there from either school or some sporting activity.' Elva had an interest in aviation which, as she says, 'gave Keith an opportunity to chat me up'. For Bennett, though, this was no easy task. He still had a speech impediment and was currently seeing a therapist to try to conquer it. While the condition predated the war, Elva believes the conflict exacerbated it. 'He had the problem before the war, but certainly some of his experiences affected him.' Bennett worked at re-building his confidence by enrolling at Sydney University to study engineering, and he took up intervarsity rowing – rowing in the four seat of the Engineering eight.

And all the while, he maintained his correspondence with Jannie, who was then in England working as an au pair. Though their relationship was never anything but platonic, Bennett apparently charmed Jannie with his letters and the little gifts he sent her. As Jannie wrote to Elva in 2006: 'I shall never forget that Keith sent me parcels with clothes in 1946 . . . and also two pairs of nylon stockings. I had never seen nylon stockings before. I was very delighted and proud wearing them.'

Bennett's courtship with Elva developed. They went on dates into the Sydney CBD to watch French films at the Savoy Theatre in Bligh Street, and would regularly visit the art gallery. One memorable night out, Elva recalls, was a dinner-dance at Carl Thomas' restaurant, located in an old warehouse in Macquarie Street. The blind pianist Julian Lee played many of the classical wartime tunes that Bennett and his crew had heard at the Village Inn in Binbrook and other Lincolnshire pubs.

Listening to the familiar tunes, Bennett was prompted to share some of his war experiences with Elva that until then he had held within. He began by recounting his memory of Cyril Entwistle's wedding in 1945, just after the war ended, and Henry Ford's marriage to Pat in late 1944 after Ford met his English-born bride-to-be in Blackpool shortly before his crew was deployed to 460 Squadron. Bennett also told Elva about the many amorous exploits of his bomb-aimer, Alby Murray. 'Hence the name "the chick magnet",' recalls Elva. She adds that it was around this time that Bennett started to deal with his grief over the loss of so many close friends during the war. As she explains, 'Keith wrote to the parents of his friends who were killed during the bombing raids over Germany instigated by "Bomber" Harris.'

Bennett's days at Sydney University were happy ones, though, and helped to forge the life that awaited him. Despite his ill-feelings about the war, the cheeky larrikin within Bennett was still very much alive, as the university's annual 'Butchers and Greasers' parade in 1948 through the streets of Sydney proved. The parade, to celebrate the end of year at the university, was always followed by a flour fight between the Butchers, who were undergraduate medical students, and Greasers, the undergraduate engineers. By now Bennett had also added sketching nudes to his increasing list of interests, and the side of the truck that he and his fellow students commanded for the parade was adorned by his own artwork. It was a giant mural of a reclining unclad girl baring all, titled 'Fanny by Gaslight' – the name a mocking reference to the wave of electrical blackouts that Sydney was experiencing at the time which left many households using gaslights as a back-up.

There was no one prouder of his contribution to the parade than Bennett. Dressed in his trademark kit of navy blue overalls and a black bowler hat, he rode with a grin from ear to ear on the back of the truck for the procession, which ended, as it did every year, with an afternoon session of drinking in the pub among fellow university students. However, so proud was Bennett of his masterpiece 'Fanny' that several hours after the celebratory swill, he dared to take 'her' to show Elva at her work in Martin Place – much to her and her fellow workers' shock, not to mention her boss's surprise.

'Keith decided to call in. He was still dressed in navy overalls and a bowler hat and proceeded to unroll this enormous poster of "Fanny" in front of about eight girls and a not-so-happy boss,' Elva recalls of a moment that became more like a scene out of a slapstick Charlie Chaplin movie than a romantic attempt by Bennett to court his wife-to-be's affections. 'As fast as he unrolled his drawing, he was being chased by its rolling up on itself,' she says.

But the humour quickly disappeared after Bennett finally succeeded in having 'Fanny' fully unravelled on the floor and open for display before the goggle-eyes of the gob-smacked audience that stood before him. 'He then embarrassed me by announcing [wrongly, that] I had posed for the poster,' says Elva.

For Elva, the incident heightened her relief that by then she had set a fresh new vocational path and had already given her employer notice.

In June 1948, Elva was accepted by Trans Australia Airways (TAA) for the next intake of air stewardesses. She moved to Melbourne for a six-week course, and afterwards was based in the Victorian state capital where she worked for three months. Though the separation wasn't easy for Bennett and Elva, they were still able to see each other fairly regularly. 'When I was passing through Sydney, Keith would be waiting at Mascot [airport]. He had no car, would come by public transport, and would only have 10 minutes to talk. I'm sure I'd be in Melbourne or Brisbane before he got back to Lane Cove,' Elva recalls.

Bennett was still in contact with most of his crew in Australia – Alby Murray, Henry Ford and Peter Firkins. Elva got the opportunity to meet Firkins, who was living in WA, when she joined the crew of a DC 6 promotional flight to Perth. Firkins was then in the Hollywood Repatriation Hospital. 'He is still the most suave fellow I have ever met, and we remained great friends,' says Elva of Firkins, who died 31 July 2001.

In 1950, Bennett graduated as an engineer and was employed at Boral at Matraville. He was by then rapidly finding his true independence, out from under the shadow of his father. It was independence helped by his ownership of a car, a second-hand Singer, the interior of which was adorned with blue felt, which he could drive around Sydney in – often with Elva in tow. He was also helping his youngest brother, Alan, establish a valve-stripping business. Bennett soon joined the business, starting a partnership between the brothers that lasted thirty years. Bennett encouraged his younger brother to take up tennis, and played Saturday squash with him, and later helped build Alan's first house, in Killara. Today, Alan observes that Bennett took on a paternal role in the relationship: 'I was the youngest one by about ten years, and he was the eldest and by then had travelled the world.' Alan also admits that it has only been in the years following his brother's death that he got a grasp on what he had endured during the war, the risks he'd faced, and the emotional impact of battle. 'He felt guilty towards the end of the war because of the bombing of Dresden and Hamburg. He felt Dresden was just for revenge, something done in spite. He felt that it wasn't really needed as the war was almost over.'

On 20 June 1950, Bennett finally took the plunge and proposed to Elva, telling her: 'If you marry me, I will build you a stone fireplace. Every day it will give me much pleasure.' A strange proposal perhaps, but he understood her passion for stonemasonry – in particular for the buildings in Macquarie Street, one of the few streets in Sydney that today still boasts some examples of the colonial architecture of the Macquarie era.

He was no doubt also aware of her father and grandfather's backgrounds as stonemasons.

For Elva, the passion was matched only by her love of cedar furniture that would see the family spend many a day off at local antique auctions.

Little wonder Elva accepted Bennett's proposal. In 1952 they were married by Reverend Ray Weir, a Scouting friend of Bennett's, at the chapel of St Andrew's Cathedral. They didn't waste time. Despite living in an era when budgets were tight and the thinking was to err on the side of caution, they immediately went on their honeymoon to Melbourne and visited Bennett's former crewmate Henry Ford and his wife, Pat. Shortly afterwards, the Bennetts started a family: their son Graham was born in 1954, followed by two daughters, Genelle in 1957 and Libby in 1962. Before long, their life seemed settled: many nights were spent at the Lane Cove home of Bennett's father and mother with singalongs around the piano. As a former member of the Birmingham Orchestra in England where he was born, not only did Bennett snr play the violin – or 'the fiddle' as he called it – but Alan's wife, Gloria, was a pianist.

As for the fireplace Bennett promised? It still stands as the centrepiece of Elva's home today.

In 1983, Bennett decided to renew his correspondence with Jannie, which had dropped off over the previous years; their last exchange had been in 1950. Bennett was due to go on a business trip to Vancouver and he hoped to visit Europe – and Jannie – on the return leg. No longer sure of Jannie's whereabouts, he began by contacting the Dutch consul in Sydney and asking for the address of her parents, Mr and Mrs G.H. Van Splunder in Ridderkerk. It was a shot in the dark but he hoped that whoever received the letter would pass it on to Jannie. He included his hotel details in Amsterdam. As he wrote:

We exchanged letters for several years after the war. I started because while flying with the RAF as a pilot I was engaged in dropping food into Rotterdam and

I dropped cigarettes with my home address on them. Unfortunately I have never been to England or Europe since the war so we have never had the opportunity to meet . . . So hopefully I would like to contact her during my visit to Holland in May. . . . If you can help with my enquiry could you please leave a message at the hotel.

The letter reached its destination. And while the recipients were not Jannie's parents, one was a cousin who was able to contact her and pass on Bennett's travel details.

Their eventual meeting with their respective partners was an emotional moment for all. Elva recalls: 'We went to their home [then in Laren], saw their beautiful garden, had afternoon tea and had dinner at a lovely restaurant. The next day we flew to London.'

Bennett remained fascinated by aviation for the rest of his life. He wrote many letters to newspapers and politicians, voicing his concerns over policy or practices within the industry, and offering his advice. While he rarely spoke of the war, he still harboured a strong conviction over what he felt were miscarriages of justice and hated to see mistakes repeated. Jannie says that on the day of their meeting in Laren, Bennett spoke of his continuing grief over the bombing of Dresden, and his steadfast opposition to Arthur Harris ordering it. 'He still had great pains about the bombardment of Dresden. He thought it was a terrible mistake of the general of the Air Force [Harris] briefing aircrews to bomb that city which resulted in so many dead citizens, as the war was already coming to an end.'

Dresden would hang heavily on Bennett's conscience for the rest of his life. It was not a subject he would discuss in groups. Jannie was privy to his thoughts, maybe because he felt she was owed an explanation, having experienced first-hand what devastation war can bring. After all, Holland had been invaded and occupied by the Nazis, and it was bombed by both the Germans and Allies who were targeting Nazi installations there. And apart from those joyous days when Operation Manna unfolded before her eyes, Jannie had become accustomed to the sight of Allied bombers flying in their hundreds – sometimes numbering 1000 – en route to and from their raids in Germany.

Bennett would also confide in his wife Elva and his children. In the closing years of his life, Bennett even spoke of his sorrow about the bombing of Dresden and other German cities to his youngest brother Alan – too young to enlist in the services during the war – who admits that until then he never really understood his brother's suffering.

Bennett was not a celebrator of war and he never marched in Anzac Day parades. However, he did attend local memorial services at the cenotaph in the grounds of Lane Cove Municipal Library, near his home, and at the Rugby Club in the city of Sydney later in the day he would charge his glass in memory of those friends and colleagues who were lost. But never one for a big show, especially a crowded pub, one of Bennett's favourite places was the Lane Cove Bowling Club – a popular haunt for many ageing veterans who preferred a quiet drink. So popular was it that it even became known as the 'Diddy' because one of the most common questions heard among the men at the bar was: 'Did he die, did he?'

Many ex-servicemen and women suffered chronic illness in the years following the war. Often these conditions went largely undiagnosed. Bennett fell victim to tuberculosis and long believed his illness stemmed from his war days. Still, he was determined to lead a full and satisfying life, and he made the most of the postwar era. One of his fondest days was in 2003 when he visited the RAAF Aviation Museum at Williamtown, New South Wales, Australia's first fighter aircraft display centre. On show was a display of planes ranging from FA 18 Hornets to the A13-211 Link Trainer, the flight simulator developed in the 1920s and still in use when Bennett's aviation days began. To make the day even more special, Bennett travelled to Williamtown by plane, a Beechcraft Bonanza that was owned and flown by his friend Rod McDonald, who granted Bennett the opportunity to take the 'stick' for a brief spell.

'Henry' Ford, Bennett's wireless operator, remembers the pledge the G2 crew made when the war ended: that they would get together every year on the same day and celebrate their time together. But they never did. 'We said all that, made the promises; but it never happened,' he says, citing the distances between them, and the myriad of circumstances – from personal health to financial footing – that made such a reunion difficult. With the exception of Englishman Cyril Entwistle, most of the crew returned home to Australia. Peter Firkins carved out a successful career in business and community affairs in Perth, as well as writing many books on the war; Alex Freezer, who had left behind his wife and two children when he enlisted, resumed his work as a sheep station manager in rural Western Australia; and Emmerson, like Ford, forged a prosperous teaching career in Victoria.

For Entwistle, there was no choice about his immediate postwar future. With the war continuing against Japan following Operation Manna, Entwistle was still available for service. He was dispatched to Catterick in the northeast of England to prepare for another tour of duty to Burma and then to India. It was a sudden change of life for Entwistle, as he recalls: 'You thought: "Last week we're all together, having a drink in the pub on the nights we were off [operations], otherwise we were flying together." Suddenly you're off on your own. God knows where you'll be posted to.'

Before farewelling his crew, Entwistle invited them to his wedding in August 1945. Though missing Emmerson and Freezer, who were already on their way home, the crew enjoyed one final reunion. The reception was a happy drunken affair, held in a pub on the Coventry by-pass. And although the whole crew was never reunited, in the years that followed most of them remained in contact and took opportunities to visit each other when they could. In 1983, Keith and Elva Bennett visited Cyril and his wife, Dorothy, at their home at the time in Warwickshire after they'd met with Jannie and Gerrit Verstigen in the Netherlands.

Of all the crew members, Bennett was closest to his bomb-aimer, Alby Murray. The two maintained a bond that lasted until Bennett's death in 2004. When Murray was applying for a disability pension, Bennett wrote him a letter of support, testifying to the physical hardship Murray endured as a bomb-aimer. It also expresses Bennett's sorrow about the devastation of war:

> Alby in 1944–45 served as bomb aimer in a Lancaster heavy bomber crew in 460 RAAF Squadron attached to RAF Bomber Command. As the pilot of this crew I wish to offer a submission in support of a review of his disability pension. Bomber Command crews were set a target of 30 bombing operations over Germany which we had the good fortune to complete when more than 50 per cent of crews did not survive. Bomber Command commander [Arthur] Harris pursued his objectives with relentless disregard for casualties. We completed 30 'ops' but most did not. German targets – cities and industrial – were defended by hundreds of anti-aircraft guns and fighters. Approaching a target, Alby lay prone in the most exposed position in the forward nose cone to observe the target and give course instructions and take photographs.

When Bennett died, Murray travelled to Sydney for the funeral at the Northern Suburbs Crematorium. Fittingly, he sat in the front row at Elva Bennett's right side, as he often did with Bennett during their operations.

As for Murray's flying days, they were well and truly over. Like Bennett, he was wary about the safety of commercial aircraft, especially as they became more and more reliant on computerised technology. 'It took me a long time to go as a passenger. I felt a bit uneasy,' he remarked years later. Today, Murray lives in a retirement village near his hometown of Maitland, 160 km north of Sydney. But he hasn't lost his spark. When I suggest to him that I write a book about the 'chick magnet' of the skies, he beams and says, 'You don't know half of it.'

Year		Aircraft		Pilot, or 1st Pilot	2nd Pilot, Pupil or Passenger	Duty (Including Results and Remarks)
Month	Date	Type	No.			
—	—	—	—	—	—	— Totals Brought Forward
May	3	Lancaster III	G²	Self	F/O Emerson	30th. Operation
					Sgt Entwistle	Supply dropping near
					F/S Murray	Rotterdam 4 blocks
					T/S Ford	of 284 sacks. 416 mls
					F/S Freezer	Weather still very
					F/S Firkins	squally

F. Lawrence S/L
O.C. 'C' Flight

_____ W/C
C.O. 460 Squadron.

SUMMARY FOR	May	TYPES.
UNIT	460 Squadron	Lancaster I
DATE	5.5.45	Lancaster III
SIGNATURE	_____	

TOTAL HOURS FOR 460 SQUADRON.

Chapter 14

Walking Back in Time

I would have nothing good to say about it.

Keith Bennett on World War II

KEITH WILLIAM BENNETT was my father-in-law. And truth be known, were he alive today the chances are that this book would not have been written. Once, when I asked Keith at a family barbecue if he would consider penning his memoirs about the war, he looked at me blankly, hesitated and responded: 'Why? I'd have nothing good to say about it.' By reading his private letters and diaries, I realise that although as a young man Keith might have romanticised war and been desperate to sign up, the experiences that followed his enlistment and eventual posting to Binbrook left him in no doubt of its destruction and enduring pain. When his tour was over, he didn't even want to speak about it.

There was, however, one operation he held close to his heart; one he was proud of – Operation Manna – as proud as the millions of starving Dutch civilians who he saved were grateful.

It was Keith's death on 25 February 2004 and subsequent funeral at the Northern Suburbs Crematorium on 4 March that year that paved the way for *The Flying Grocer* to be written. I was asked to give a eulogy at the funeral, and I based it on a brief account of Keith's disdain for the war, yet his inner pride for having played a role in Operation Manna. I talked about his chance union with Jannie Van Splunder after she found his address on a package dropped from their Lancaster bomber and included an edited extract from the first letter Jannie wrote to Keith, dated Ridderkerk, Holland, 22 February 1946, which Keith replied to, setting off the life-long friendship that still exists between the two families today.

The real catalyst for the book came when Ian Macintosh, a family friend and a former senior vice president of CNN International (Asia Pacific), approached me immediately after the service. 'It would make a great documentary,' he said. The seed was planted.

It took some time for the seed to grow and blossom, and turn from being an idea into a draft manuscript and into this book. The idea for it came and went – and came and went again – before returning with substance during a pre-Christmas lunch in Sydney in December 2005 with my mother-in-law, Elva Bennett, and my wife, Libby. Elva, who since Bennett's death had been finding more and more of her husband's stored papers, diaries and old news clippings and photographs, suddenly revealed her joy that one of the letters he had received from Jannie's best friend, Bouwine Van Vliet, had begun: 'Dear Flying Grocer . . . '

Staring me in the face was a working title, but the hard part was figuring out how to tell the story of a man who was not alive to speak for himself and who, while having been a decorated member of the Royal Australian Air Force, had hardly been known as a colourful raconteur of wartime stories. Keith was more a hoarder of pained memories that, for the most part, he wrestled with and kept to himself right up until the day he died at the age of 80.

A call to arms was needed, and I asked family members and friends to delve into their files in search for any documentation of Keith's life, from his childhood to his days during the war and after. A plan was put in place to track down and speak with any surviving members of Keith's crew. Most importantly, contact needed to be made with Jannie, with a view to arranging a meeting with her in the Netherlands and, if possible, returning to the exact landmark outside her old home village of Ridderkerk where, on 1 May 1945, Keith and Alby Murray dropped their hastily wrapped package with their addresses and a note attached.

And then came my own need to research Operation Manna, a process that prompted me to realise that Australia's role in the ten days of food-drops – let alone the uniqueness of Keith and Jannie's union through it – was something that has passed with relatively little recognition: when citing great moments of Australia's armed services in World War II, most people recall battles, not humanitarian feats like this.

With any major project, finding a place to start beyond a Google search can be hard; especially when trying to find first-hand undocumented material. And for that 'start', my best resource was Elva, who not only located and passed on to me the vital documentation I would need to start writing – things like Keith's official RAAF flight log, personal diary, photos and bundles of original newspaper clippings from the war period that he had kept stored away – but also the original letters that he had received from Jannie and Bouwine Van Vliet. That Elva was also able to speak so openly and frankly about the 'Flying Grocer' story, and to share her recollections and private thoughts of a man whom she met and married after the war and who had mostly kept his war memories to himself, was invaluable.

Elva gave me valued insights and arranged meetings with those who knew Keith and are such major characters in his story – in particular his surviving crewmates Alby Murray, Henry Ford and Cyril Entwistle, and, of course, Jannie, with whom Elva still regularly corresponds today.

Another important character in the story is Henk Benness. A neighbour and friend of the Bennett family in Sydney, Benness is Dutch and a survivor of the war – he lived through the *'Hongerwinter'* of 1944–45 when he was a 13-year-old boy from the country village of Gouda. It was by chance that Benness met Keith in the first place and discovered, while they were flipping sausages on a barbecue and chatting about their backgrounds, that fate had brought them together once before. For as they spoke, their conversation revealed Benness had been a recipient of the food-drops supplied by Keith in his role as an RAAF pilot on Bomber Command.

It was Benness who, during a meeting at the Bennett home arranged by Elva in early 2005, first brought home to me the sheer emotion and gratitude that the Dutch still feel for Operation Manna. The sight of his welling eyes nearly 60 years on as he recalled the Lancasters flying from the horizon towards him and his fellow Dutch said it all.

It caught both Elva and me unawares. She looked at me. I looked at her. She rushed off for more cupcakes. I looked back at Henk, who, to my relief, had composed himself again.

His subsequent insights and the uniqueness of his own tale of starvation and struggle in the war were as good a start in the search for fresh material as anyone could hope for.

It also provided me with the living and real passion and emotion for a tragic subject that cannot be communicated to the ignorant reader through history books and periodicals.

It was emotion, I found, that I would need to be equipped with if I was to make best use of the minimal time (12 days) that I had for a research trip to the Netherlands and England. It was a trip that fittingly – and entirely coincidentally – enveloped the period of Operation Manna, from 25 April to 6 May. That I was re-visiting a chapter of World War II history nearly 61 years to the day later, was something I only realised when I was standing at the viaduct outside Ridderkerk on 27 April, a cloudless, crisp and sunny spring day, with Jannie and her daughter Madeleine. With my video camera rolling, I asked Jannie to recall the moment on 1 May 1945 when she saw the Lancasters of 460 Squadron and others from Bomber Command flying so low above the ground from Rotterdam towards her and her friend Bouwine Van Vliet.

To hear Jannie speak so freely belied the fact we had only met for the first time a few hours earlier at the train station in Hilversum, the town where she now lives and one of the sites of the Operation Manna food-drops.

We had recognised each other at first sight: Jannie equipped with a 10-year-old photo of me at my wedding, me with one of her as an 18-year-old during the war. Whether from having heard so much about Jannie from Elva Bennett, or from having read her letters to Keith, it was as if I had known her for years as she served me chocolate cake and coffee and we sat and chatted over piles of her saved letters from Keith and re-written volumes of her personal wartime diaries at her home, before driving to Ridderkerk with her daughter.

While driving the 90 minutes south to Ridderkerk, past fields where fresh crops grew and cattle grazed steadily, oblivious to the traffic passing, Jannie's memories came flooding back to her with remarkable clarity. Even as we arrived in Ridderkerk, it was as if she had been transported back to 1945, as she pointed to the site of her old family home from which she and her parents were evicted by the Germans, then to where her father's old office had been and where they were forced to live for the last six weeks of the war. We drove through the now developed town that is twice the size it was in 1945. Jannie was bewildered when her mind returned to the present and realised how Ridderkerk had changed.

Finally, we came to the street with the building in which Jannie and Bouwine had been taking typing lessons when they first heard the deafening roar of the Lancaster Merlin engines closing in. Then we arrived at the place where this story all began: the viaduct where Keith's Lancaster dropped that package of cigarettes – and their note saying *'Naar U'* ['To you'] – before giving the airman's wave and signalling off with a dip of his wings.

As Jannie spoke of the drop and what Operation Manna meant to her, I recalled the emotions of Henk Benness back in Australia. And as I discovered in the days to come, whenever anyone spoke of Operation Manna the emotions were the same.

And such strong feelings were not exclusive to those who had survived the war. As Jannie finished recounting her memories of the supply-drop, I turned and was greeted by the sight of her daughter Madeleine softly crying.

Returning by car to Hilversum for the train trip back to Amsterdam, the spring sun dimming on the horizon, it was as if I had been caught in a time warp and taken back to 1945. So vivid were Jannie's recollections at Ridderkerk and in the car, where she continued to speak of her family, her first meeting with her future husband, Gerrit Verstigen, and her hopes and dreams for her life for the remainder of the war and after it.

Jannie also spoke of her close friend Bouwine from Rotterdam, who had lived with the Van Splunders during the German occupation because her family could not feed her due to food shortages that struck the cities first. I decided to visit Rotterdam both in light of Bouwine's background, and because it was the bombing of Rotterdam on 14 May 1940 that triggered the Battle of Holland and led to the German occupation.

Rotterdam – like many Dutch cities – became a major centre for the rounding up of Jews and their dispersal to work and concentration camps, as well as becoming a hub for the Dutch Resistance.

Perhaps fittingly, a grey and cloudy sky hung over Rotterdam as I arrived. As with many ancient and beautiful cities that were bombed to destruction in the war, the biggest sign of the devastation Rotterdam sustained is its reconstruction into a concrete maze of modern-style buildings that are merciless to the eye. But there is a lot more that mirrors the suffering Rotterdam experienced in the war than the impersonal architecture that remains.

Inspired by Jannie's account of her husband's past as a member of the Dutch Resistance, I walked south from Rotterdam Centraal Station, towards the Nieuwe Maas River, which I crossed via the Erasmusburg Bridge, to the Oorlogs Verzets Museum – or Dutch Resistance Museum. Initially set up to commemorate the bombing of Rotterdam, the museum is located on the southwestern side of the bridge in the Kattendrecht district, a drab dockland area largely populated by African immigrants. Housed in a nondescript converted house, bare of any sign indicating what it is, I walked past the museum twice before realising it was what I was looking for.

The Oorlogs Verzets Museum is more than a fine tribute to the Dutch Resistance: it is a memorial to the Netherlands' experiences throughout the war. Included in a room-to-room self-guided tour are myriad displays of re-created period scenes, complete with costumed mannequins, historic photos and other wartime memorabilia depicting the Battle of the Netherlands, the bombing of Rotterdam, the air war that followed, the German occupation, the role of the merchant navy, the use of propaganda, the persecution of the Jews, the creation and impact of underground press, the workings of the Resistance and finally the Liberation.

One of the more powerful displays is the music room, which visitors reach at the end of their tour. Music played such a pivotal role in buoying spirits during the war and in this room many of the wartime classics, in many languages, can be heard on headsets. For English-speaking visitors, the all-time greats are available – from Glenn Miller's 'Moonlight Serenade', Vera Lynn's 'We'll Meet Again', Marlene Dietrich's recording of 'Lili Marleen', and The Ramblers' 'Farewell Blues', to many, many more from the likes of Marlene Dietrich, Anne Shelton and Gracie Fields.

And as on many a visit in this trip, the mere mention of Operation Manna, 460 Squadron and that my father-in-law was a Flying Officer who had piloted a Lancaster bomber crew that took part in the food-drops, drew immediate interest from those who asked what I was researching just as I was about to leave the museum. Then, after politely declining the invitation from six ageing locals to join in a singalong of those wartime classics, I couldn't help but suspect they knew a great deal more about what war was like than I ever will.

From the Oorlogs Verzets Museum, my journey took me east to where Shed 24 had stood during the war. It was here where the Jews were ordered to congregate before being transported to work and concentration camps throughout Europe. The site is now a grassed square that sits morbidly in the towering shadows of three modern apartment blocks. A small mobile construction office and a portaloo stood to the left of the small sign that read 'Shed 24' in Dutch.

Further east and following the Nieuwe Maas River along Stieltjes Straat, along which the Jews began their doomed journeys, there is little to lift spirits. After crossing a small bridge named the Koninginnebrug, which connects the south bank to the Noordereiland in the middle of the Nieuwe Maas River, the Willemsburg Bridge soon comes into sight: 100 metres east of the new modern steel version stand the stanchions of the once statuesque old bridge that was blasted away in the Luftwaffe's mass bombing of Rotterdam on 14 May and never re-built.

Near the foot of the old bridge I looked at a colourful mosaic showing children's depictions of Rotterdam's bombing, along with several other key moments in local history that include Holland's flooding during the war, the city's reconstruction and celebration with the Liberation. Then I headed to the new bridge for the walk back to Centraal Station.

I looked up to the skies of Rotterdam as I crossed, trying to imagine what it might have been like in 1945 as the frightening spectre of German planes suddenly appeared to drop their bombs.

The thought haunted me all the way back to Centraal Station, as I realised from the modern architecture of Rotterdam's inner-city buildings that most of the streets I was walking through had met a similar fate to the Willemsburg Bridge.

Emotionally drained, on the train back to Amsterdam I was grateful that the next day – 29 April – was a day of celebration for the Dutch Queen's birthday. And celebrate the Dutch do on this day, like no other country I have witnessed, with inner-city Amsterdam awash in Dutch orange, the canals overflowing with a frenzy of floating parties, and every nook and cranny filled to the brim with festivity. Later that night I realised it was 61 years to the day after Operation Manna officially began with Keith Bennett happily flying out on his first of three sorties in the mission.

The next day, looking down on the steely blue waters of the English Channel from my seat on a British Airways flight, I thought about Keith and how he and his crew must have been feeling one day shy of 61 years before, when they had completed their second of three food-drops, the one that led to Keith and Alby Murray dropping their parcel over Ridderkerk. Dared I even try to imagine what they felt? The world as we know it has changed so much since then, and, whether fair or not, war is rarely something Australians of my generation have experienced first-hand. But after the emotions of the previous days in Holland and inspired by a desire to try to recapture what Keith and his crew experienced, I threw caution to the wind.

So . . . as Holland paled into the horizon behind me and England draws near, I imagined the warmth the crew must have felt knowing they and their colleagues had helped save thousands of lives; their joy from seeing the waving arms, smiles and cheers of the Dutch survivors on the ground who received the food and supply parcels; and the relief of all on either side of the Channel that World War II was finally at an end.

Up until Operations Manna and Chowhound were carried out by the Allies, crews knew that each crossing of the Channel by a plane en route to or from another massive bombing raid over Europe could well be their last. And in the case of Keith's crew, I thought how fortunate they were to complete their tour with all on board safe and sound and able to look ahead to a lifetime of peace.

Of course, I knew all too well that there were thousands of others who were not as fortunate; especially in 460 Squadron, who suffered the greatest casualties, despite being the most decorated squadron, and boasting the greatest number of raids and bomb-drops of any in Bomber Command. I also knew that those like Bennett and his crew who did survive realised that plain and cold fact even better than anyone else.

Countless anecdotes I had read in preparation for this trip flooded back. There were stories of those who survived those raids, and those who did not. There were tales of the battles that had been fought over the Channel waters, above me and below; as well as back in Europe where the German Luftwaffe was a constant and frightening threat. There were even anecdotes of the Allied bombers reaching the supposedly safe skies above England, only to find German fighters waiting to exact what they felt was due punishment for the Allies' brazen and sometimes controversial bombing raids that were so crucial in bringing to an end the war. I turned around from my seat to see if I could catch a last glimpse of Europe as it faded into the horizon, attempting to get an inkling of relief crews felt in day raids as they flew away from the mushrooms of smoke left in their wake.

What must it have felt like to fly away from England? To see the green pastures and church steeples disappear from sight as the Lancasters charged headlong into enemy skies, where the only welcome they would get would be the blinding flash of 'flak' from the ack-ack guns and searchlights below. Then would have come the swarms of German fighters, swooping from the left, right and below as they tried to shoot the Allies down before their bomb bays opened to drop another massive load of explosive firepower that would wreak havoc and death.

Add to that the horror of seeing fellow Bomber Command Lancasters collide in mid-air – if they were not shot down – and go down in balls of flames, knowing that if the crews managed to escape from the plane alive and parachute jump, their options were to be captured by the Germans and live out the war in a prisoner of war camp, or sneak back into Allied territory, return to base and risk their lives in battle again.

Later that morning Keith's flight engineer, Cyril Entwistle, met me at Coventry station and as he drove me to his home in Kenilworth, Warwickshire, he spoke of the devastation of Coventry during the war, when the Germans obliterated the city with their bombing raids. Our chat continued over tea and biscuits at his two-storey, semi-detached townhouse and then over a pint of lager and lunch at the local pub. Cyril talked about Bennett, the G2 crew, 460 Squadron, Binbrook and the rights and wrongs of the war.

When I noticed he was not eating, Cyril confided that since his wife Dorothy died he had lost his appetite. There was an uncomfortable pause, and then Cyril's eyes lit up once again. He laughed, recalling another anecdote, another tale from war. He had not forgotten – the good or the bad.

When we parted ways at the train station a few hours later – with my train pulling out for Lincoln – there was a tinge of sadness. As the farming fields of Bomber County started to pass me by, I realised that while the war may have been long over and the once constant drone of bombers and shrill of fighter planes above were no more, for Cyril, living where it was fought, the war had not gone.

Neither has the war gone from Bomber County – or Lincolnshire – especially at Binbrook where 460 Squadron was based and the towns in its environs like Market Rasen. Although the airbase that was home to so many great squadrons closed in 1985, you only need walk across the vacant runway, close your eyes and breathe the stiff winds that blow from the North Sea to feel what it must have been like for 460 Squadron. In the haze, two kilometres away, the steeple of St Mary and St Gabriel Church stands proudly, almost boasting its importance in war not just as the beacon of a safe haven during war for a distressed population, but literally as a beacon for returning crews.

Walk into Binbrook village today and the spirit is as strong. There is the memorial for 460 Squadron at the village entrance, and the stained-glass window inside St Mary's bears the insignia of every squadron that made Binbrook home. There are the memories of Binbrook locals who have not forgotten – and never will – the sacrifice made by those who made the village in the Lincolnshire 'wolds' their last home.

The Marquis of Granby is no longer a pub but now a heritage home. Long gone are the days when it would be full to the rafters with airmen – often literally. It was a tradition in pubs throughout Lincolnshire (albeit not always followed) that an airman who completed his tour of 30 operations would be held aloft by fellow drinkers to sign his name on the ceiling.

Visiting Binbrook today, it is easy to understand the financial impact that having an airbase there had, not just on the village but on the entire surrounding region.

After the war, there were fewer customers at local pubs, restaurants, cafes, hotels, shops and demand for local transport services dropped off, so in time tourism and farming increased. Tourism is still a major industry for the county today, as Lincolnshire almost trades on its wartime label as Bomber County. The most common subject of all the books, tea towels and other wartime memorabilia available in the area is Lincolnshire's role in World War II.

The county achieved a degree of posterity – and indeed prosperity – when Binbrook airbase was chosen as a film location for the 1990 Hollywood adaptation of the Willy Wyler-directed documentary *Memphis Belle*. This was the story of a USAF B17 Flying Fortress crew piloted by Robert Morgan on its 25th and final mission of the war.

For three months, Lincolnshire was swamped by the cast and crew of the movie, who booked out the local pubs, bed and breakfasts, restaurants and hotels.

One such establishment was the Limes County Hotel, where the production crew stayed, and to which a very shaken explosives expert returned one evening during the shoot after being the first on the scene to drag out the crews when two of the stunt planes had collided.

Hearing that anecdote made me wonder what it must have been like during the war, when tragedies would have been reported nightly and bars across the county would have been as packed in commiseration for lost mates as they were for the celebration of having survived another operation.

Although I could never really comprehend what Keith, his crew and the thousands who flew in Bomber Command – or even enlisted and fought in any war – felt, my visit to Lincolnshire gave me a greater understanding of Keith's negative response when I asked him if he would ever consider writing his memoirs.

Maybe through Keith's open disdain for the war he was simply trying to close the door on anyone who had never experienced or fought in war ever wanting to. What is clear from the private letters and diaries Keith left behind after his death was that although he had been desperate to sign up, by the time his tour was over he knew there was no romance in war.

We, in his family, knew the inner tussle Keith had with his conscience over the role he played in the devastation and death caused by the raids of Bomber Command whose push into Germany turned the war in the Allies' favour.

But we also knew, without him talking about it, that there was one operation Keith and his crew were deeply proud of, and even happier that they could end their war by being a part of it: Operation Manna, one of the greatest but (in Australia) most under-acknowledged humanitarian war efforts ever staged.

I still wonder how Keith would have answered so many of the questions I wish I could have asked him about the war and, in particular, Operation Manna. I must admit that I wonder if he would have really agreed with what I have written. I can only say that I hope so. But more importantly, in the absence of Keith's first-hand version of the story of the 'Flying Grocer', I hope this account will bring due recognition to him and to all those who took part in a mission that not only saved millions from death, but which lit up the dark years of war with a sense of optimism and hope for those brave airmen.

YEAR		AIRCRAFT		Pilot, or 1st Pilot	2nd Pilot, Pupil or Passenger	DUTY (Including Results and Remarks)
Month	Date	Type	No.			
—	—	—		—	—	— Totals Brought Forward
May	3	LANCASTER III	G₂	SELF	F/O EMERSON	30TH. OPERATION
					SGT ENTWISTLE	SUPPLY DROPPING NEAR
					F/S MURRAY	ROTTERDAM. 4 BLOCKS
					T/S FORD	OF 284 SACKS. 416 MLS
					T/S FREEZER	WEATHER STILL. VERY
					F/S FIRKINS	SQUALLY

F. Lawrence S/L
O.C. 'C' FLIGHT

_____ W/C.
C.O. 460 SQUADRON.

SUMMARY FOR. May
UNIT   460 SQUADRON
DATE   5·5·45
SIGNATURE _____

TYPES.
LANCASTER I
LANCASTER III

TOTAL HOURS FOR 460 SQUADRON.

Chapter 15

A Father's Message

THROUGHOUT WORLD WAR II AND THE YEARS AFTER, Keith Bennett kept in his personal diary a small slip of faded yellow paper upon which is neatly typed Rudyard Kipling's poem 'If'. His father had given it to him before he left Australia to serve.

The poem, written in 1895 and first published in Kipling's *Rewards and Fairies* in 1909, was inspired by Dr Leander Starr Jameson. Jameson led a British assault of about 500 men against the Boers in South Africa that later became known as the 'Jameson Run'.

Despite losing the battle, Jameson was hailed as a hero.

The poem contains words of advice that no doubt inspired Bennett during his war years. Indeed, many have been and continue to be motivated by its message of humility and grace under pressure.

If

If you can keep your head when all about you
Are losing theirs, and blaming it on you;
If you can trust yourself when all men doubt you,
But make allowance for their doubting too,
If you can wait and not be tired by waiting,
Or being lied about, don't deal in lies,
Or being hated, don't give way to hating
And yet, don't look too good nor talk too wise.

If you can dream – and not make dreams your master;
If you can think – and not make thoughts your aim;
If you can meet with Triumph, and Disaster
And treat those two imposters, just the same;
If you can bear to hear the truth you've spoken
Twisted by knaves to make a trap for fools,
Or watch the things you gave your life to broken,
And stoop and build 'em up with worn-out tools.

If you can make one heap of all your winnings
And risk it on one turn of pitch-and-toss,
And lose, and start again at your beginnings
And never breathe a word, about your loss;
If you can force your heart and nerve and sinew
To serve your turn long after they have gone,
And so hold on when there is nothing in you
Except the Will which says to them 'Hold on.'

A Father's Message

If you can talk with crowds and keep your virtue,
Or walk with Kings – nor lose the common touch,
If neither foes nor loving can hurt you,
If all men count with you, but none too much;
If you can fill the unforgiving minute
With sixty seconds' worth of distance run,
Yours is the Earth and everything that's in it,

And – which is more – you'll be a Man my son!

YEAR		AIRCRAFT		Pilot, or 1st Pilot	2nd Pilot, Pupil or Passenger	DUTY (Including Results and Remarks)
Month	Date	Type	No.			
—	—	—	—	—	—	Totals Brought Forward
May	3	Lancaster III	G2	SELF	F/O Emerson	30TH. OPERATION
					Sgt Entwistle	SUPPLY DROPPING NEAR
					F/S Murray	ROTTERDAM 4 BLOCKS
					F/S Ford	OF 284 SACKS. 416 MLS
					F/S Freezer	WEATHER STILL VERY
					F/S Firkins	SQUALLY

F. Lawrence S/L
O.C. 'C' Flight

~~[signature]~~ W/c.
C.O. 460 Squadron.

SUMMARY FOR May   TYPES.
UNIT   460 Squadron   LANCASTER I
DATE   5.5.45   LANCASTER III
SIGNATURE [signature]

TOTAL HOURS FOR 460 SQUADRON.

Acknowledgements

Every book written only compounds my belief that an author will always need help, and my appreciation that so many are so giving of that help.

This book is a case in point. First and foremost, my gratitude is due to my father-in-law, Keith Bennett DFC, who, was the source of inspiration for it to be written, ironically due to his silence about the war. But on equal footing I must also include his wife and my mother-in-law, Elva, whose openness and help, strength and inspiration has been endless, and her children Libby (my wife), Graham, Genelle and her partner, Mark Hobart, who were constants with their support, input with anecdotes and who facilitated many of the interviews I carried out with Bennett's surviving crew and their families.

Of course, no page of acknowledgements would be complete without special mention of Jannie Verstigen who from the Netherlands not only remained in close contact with Keith and Elva Bennett after the war, but is today a close family friend. Jannie's heartwarming story is as courageous as anyone's in this book. Ditto for Henk Benness, today the Bennetts' neighbour, but during the war – like Jannie – one of millions who were struggling day-in, day-out to survive. Henk, thank you for your story and being so open with your expression that put me on the right path.

The same must be said of Bennett's crewmates on the G2 Lancaster of 460 Squadron. Australians, as much as the Dutch, are indebted to them for their sacrifices and efforts during the war. And to those who were alive to help me in writing this book – Alby Murray, Cyril Entwistle, and Harold 'Henry' Ford, and their families – a million 'thank yous' would not even come close to my gratitude for your time and frank appraisal and reflections of such a turbulent and tragic period.

As deserving of my thanks are the children and partners whom I have spoken to and sought help from. In particular, I refer to Jannie's daughter Madeleine; Alby Murray's daughters Sharon, Janet, Robin, Catherine, Janet and Louise; and Henry Ford's wife, Pat. Ditto for Laurie Woods DFC, Harry and Jeff Dunne, Peter McGrath and Belinda Gillies, whose help was crucial. This book could not have been written without their assistance and insight. I know that my intrusion to their lives and questioning over what were extremely personal issues was sudden and, at times, my requests may have appeared demanding. I was always in awe as to how willing, co-operative and honest they all were, not only in their responses, but also with their supply of letters, documents, photographs and advice that have helped to make this a more vivid account.

It would certainly be remiss not to thank Air Chief Marshal Angus Houston AO, AFC for his thoughts and words that he wrote for the foreword. World War II may be long past but the efforts and sacrifices of our Defence Forces in Australia are as deserving of our recognition now as then.

Of course, my parents' support and interest have been extremely appreciated. Thanks must go to my father, Perry; mother, Daphne; step-mother, Consuelo; and step-father, Robin. They may suspect their parental advice may sometimes go wanting, but trust me, it is taken in and hopefully they see how.

Finally, to Random House Australia, all I can say is thanks again for your faith.

To senior publisher Jeanne Ryckmans and senior editor Jessica Dettmann, thanks for your drive and advice. To editor Nadine Davidoff, once more you have done wonders in the edit. Thanks to Darian Causby for the cover design of the book, and to production co-ordinator Lisa Shillan. And thanks to publicist Annabel Rijks for preparing *The Flying Grocer* for take-off. May it reach dizzy heights.

And to all my friends, what can I say but thanks for being exactly that – friends.

My last word of gratitude goes to all those who have served in 460 Squadron:

May you always be remembered.

YEAR		AIRCRAFT		Pilot, or	2nd Pilot. Pupil	DUTY
Month	Date	Type	No.	1st Pilot	or Passenger	(Including Results and Remarks)
—	—	—	—	—	—	— Totals Brought Forward
May	3	Lancaster III	G₂	Self	F/O Emerson	30TH. OPERATION
					Sgt Entwistle	Supply dropping near
					F/S Murray	Rotterdam. 4 blocks
					T/S Ford	of 284 sacks. 416 mls
					F/S Freezer	Weather still very
					F/S Firkins	squally

F. Laurence, S/L
O.C. 'C' Flight

W/C
C.O. 460 Squadron.

SUMMARY FOR May.
UNIT   460 Squadron
DATE   5.5.45
SIGNATURE

TYPES.
Lancaster I
Lancaster III

TOTAL HOURS FOR 460 SQUADRON.

Bibliography

Books

Paul Addison and Jeremy A. Crang, *Firestorm*, Pimlico, 2006

Edward Davidson and Dale Manning, *World War Two – The Personalities*, Arms and Armour Press, 1997

P.A Donker, *Winter '44–'45 in Holland*, A.D. Donker Publishing, 1945

Peter Firkins, *Heroes have Wings*, Hesperian Press, 1993

Peter Firkins, *Strike and Return*, Westward Ho, 1985

M. Garbet & B. Goulding, *Lancaster*, PRC Publishing, 1971 and 1979

Hank Nelson, *Chased by the Sun*, Allen & Unwin, 2006

Hans Onderwater, *Memories of a Miracle – Operation Manna/Chowhound*, A.D. Donker, 1995

John Herington, *Australia in the War of 1939–45 – Air Power over Europe 1944–45*, Australian War Memorial, 1963

Laurie Woods DFC, *Flying into the Mouth of Hell*, Australian Military History Pubs, 2003

Magazines

Aviation Monthly, June 1995 (IPC Magazines/UK)

Imperial War Museum (London/UK)

Wartime, Issue 19 (Nuance Multimedia/Aus)

Websites and Museums

460 Squadron – www.460squadronraaf.com

Peter Dunn's Australia @ War – www.OZATWAR.com

Royal British Legion (Paris branch) – ww.rblfrance.org

Australian War Memorial, Canberra – www.awm.gov.au

Imperial War Museum, London – www.iwm.org.uk

Letters, newspaper cuttings and documents courtesy of:

Jannie Verstigen

Elva Bennett

Alby Murray

Year		Aircraft		Pilot, or 1st Pilot	2nd Pilot, Pupil or Passenger	Duty (Including Results and Remarks)
Month	Date	Type	No.			
—	—	—	—	—	—	—— Totals Brought Forward
May	3	Lancaster III	G₂	Self	F/O Emerson	30th. Operation
					Sgt Entwistle	Supply dropping near
					F/S Murray	Rotterdam. 4 blocks
					T/S Ford	of 284 sacks. 416 mls
					F/S Freezer	Weather still. very
					F/S Firkins	squally

F. Lawrence S/L
O.C. "C" Flight

				Summary for. May		Types.
				Unit	460 Squadron	Lancaster I
				Date.	5-5-45	Lancaster III.
		W/C.		Signature	R.W.B_____ts	

C.O. 460 Squadron.

Total Hours For 460 Squadron.

About the Author

Rupert Guinness is a Walkley Award commended senior sports writer who writes for the *Sydney Morning Herald* and who has covered 15 Tours de France. He is a former editor of *Winning Bicycle Racing Illustrated* magazine, European correspondent for *VeloNews* (USA) and a contributor to *Cycling Weekly* (UK) and *Velo* (France). He is also the author of seven books on cycling including *Aussie Aussie Aussie, Oui!, Oui! Oui!*, *The Foreign Legion, Tales From the Toolbox: Inside a Pro Cycling Team* and *The Dean Woods Manual of Cycling*. Rupert, who lives in Sydney, also writes on rugby union and rowing and has covered two Olympic Games.